Cat Tales

CAT TALES

Text by Emily Kearns

An Hachette UK Company
www.hachette.co.uk

Summersdale Publishers Ltd
Part of Octopus Publishing Group Limited
Carmelite House
50 Victoria Embankment
LONDON
EC4Y 0DZ
UK

www.summersdale.com

Printed and bound in Malaysia

ISBN: 978-1-83799-282-9

Substantial discounts on bulk quantities of Summersdale books are available to corporations, professional associations and other organizations. For details contact general enquiries: telephone: +44 (0) 1243 771107 or email: enquiries@summersdale.com.

Cat Tales

COMFORTING STORIES OF
FAITHFUL FELINE FRIENDS

Ashley Morgan

summersdale

CONTENTS

INTRODUCTION

This uplifting collection of stories goes to show what many of us already know: that our feline friends are some of life's most steadfast companions. So many of the cats featured in these pages have given their owners or rescuers unwavering loyalty, comfort and support, having a huge and sometimes life-changing impact on these people's day-to-day existence.

There are the cats who care, providing friendship for the lonely, comfort to the sick and tending to humans or animals in their hour of need.

Then there are the superhero cats, capable of everything from rescuing their owners from diabetic comas to sensing danger, whether in the form of an intruder, a volcanic eruption or a dangerous animal attack.

There are also the famous cats, from social media stars to those owned and cared for by world leaders either as pets or pest controllers, finding themselves in the public eye and having their every move scrutinized by the public and press.

But, above all, they are often simply members of the family who brighten up a home setting and return the love they receive in the best way they know how.

BANDIT: THE GUARD CAT

Fred Everitt was a retiree living in Tupelo, Mississippi, USA, with his adopted cat Bandit, whom he met at the Tupelo-Lee Humane Society four years previously. The home Fred shared with his calico cat was in the suburb of Belden and one July night in 2022, they had unexpected visitors.

In the early hours, Fred was awoken by Bandit meowing loudly in the kitchen downstairs. Bandit then ran upstairs and started pulling the blankets from Fred's bed before jumping on top of him – quite a force to reckon with given her 9.1 kilogram weight! Bandit then clawed at Fred's arms to get his attention.

Fred realized something must be wrong for Bandit to be acting so out of character, so got out of bed to investigate. He saw two young men outside his back door trying to break in. One held a handgun, while the other was trying to pry the door open with a crowbar.

The sight of movement inside the house clearly spooked the would-be intruders as, by the time Fred had returned to the kitchen with a weapon of his own, they had fled.

Fred said: "You hear of guard dogs. This is a guard cat. It did not turn into a confrontational situation, thank goodness, but I think that's only because of the cat."

Bandit's story was shared on social media and prompted users to share their own stories of family feline heroism. One woman credited her cat Jaxxon with being a "hero" and told how one night he had woken her very quietly to let her know there were people in the house. With her two daughters in her bedroom, she shut the door and the family were left alone.

BARNEY: THE MUSICAL CAT

Barney became an unlikely TikTok sensation when his owner uploaded a video of him playing a keyboard. Musicians on social media took note.

The ginger cat lives with his musician human Marsel Gilmanov in Moscow, who every now and again likes to join his feline friend in a duet. Barney uses his front paws to gently push the keys in a style many have likened to experimental jazz.

Following the introduction of TikTok's Duet feature, musicians using the video-sharing social media site have been able to layer their own accompaniment over Barney's riffs to collaborate with the talented mog. And while the height of Barney's TikTok fame came during the time of pandemic-related restrictions, this clever function enables musicians to virtually collaborate with anyone on the site – even musical animals.

While Barney's efforts at improv jazz might seem a little sparse on their own, they really come to life when others step in and follow Barney's musical lead in order to add something to the mix and enhance the tune. While @akizguitar added some classical guitar, it wasn't long before a third collaborator, vocalist @egglemonade, contributed to the mix by adding a lounge vibe and really strengthening the mood. Bassist Jeffin Rodegheri also wanted a piece of the action and layered some four-string stylings over Barney's experimental plinking.

Barney's videos feature on his owner's account @mars.gilmanov, which has thousands of followers – who, let's face it, are here for the cat. Most of the videos on offer capture Barney tinkling on the electronic ivories – which really is a sight worth seeing. He's brought such joy to so many in the social media community that one wonders if he could be the first cat to win an Ivor Novello Award.

BART: BACK FROM THE DEAD

Bart was a cat that certainly made people think about the nine lives theory. When the black-and-white cat from Tampa, Florida, was hit by a car one night in 2015, his owner was sure he had died in the accident. The owner decided to bury his pet, but five days later Bart re-emerged – injured, matted and hungry.

Poor Bart had a broken jaw, a ruptured eye and was covered in cuts and bruises. He was dehydrated and meowing for food, but he was definitely alive. His owner assumed Bart had regained consciousness after being buried in a shallow grave and had somehow managed to claw his way out.

Bart was rushed to the Humane Society of Tampa Bay where his damaged eye was removed, his jaw was wired and he was given a feeding tube.

After his miraculous rescue, word spread across the internet of the "zombie cat" who had returned from the dead to live out another of his nine lives. Cat lovers the world over were moved by Bart's remarkable tale of bravery and donations flooded in from all corners of the globe. Bart's medical bills came to a whopping $11,000, but with $9,000 in donations and the rest kindly covered by the Humane Society, he was on the road to recovery.

The Humane Society's executive director Sherry Silk said: "How many cats can crawl out of a grave? He deserves it.

I can't even imagine how he must have felt. He's just a really wonderful, patient, loving cat."

Bart's story doesn't end there. As he recovered from his injuries and the time drew near for him to return home to his owner, extra details about Bart's accident and burial began to emerge.

The Humane Society decided that under no circumstances should Bart return to his previous life, issuing the following statement: "We are prepared to fight for the best interests of this cat. We hope the family will do the right thing and surrender Bart to our care so that we can find an appropriate environment for him to live out his life."

A legal battle followed as the owner fought for his cat and the Humane Society fought for Bart's future well-being. The shelter refused to give up, however, and after $5,000 in legal fees and 20 months, the Humane Society decided to offer the owner $5,000 for full custody of the life-loving cat.

A member of staff at the shelter who had been fostering Bart immediately offered to adopt him, making him a permanent member of her family along with her two other cats with whom Bart soon got along famously.

After the legal resolution, Sherry said: "This cat has a spirit like no other and he was determined to live."

BEAU: IMPECCABLE BEDSIDE MANNER

David adopted Beau for mutual companionship, but never dreamed of the role his new cat would go on to play in his life.

He knew she was special when he first laid eyes on her at the Cats Protection shelter. No other cat had been living at the shelter for as long as Beau – she was overweight and had a heart murmur. An eight-year-old tortoiseshell, she was considered an older feline and the search for a forever home for her had been something of a struggle. David, who lives in Carmarthenshire in Wales, said: "She had been passed up by lots of people, but something about her caught my eye."

Eighteen months after Beau came to live with him, David was diagnosed with an incurable blood cancer. After his diagnosis, Beau began to follow him around the house, refusing to leave his side. She would remain as close to him as she possibly could and on the days when he couldn't leave his bed she was there to comfort him by nuzzling up to him and purring. If his breathing became shallow while he was asleep, Beau would bat David's face with her paw to wake him up and make sure he was OK. David was grateful that his feline companion gave him "something to focus on" during an extremely difficult time.

Beau's caring bedside manner has led David to nickname her his "fluffy nurse". Before his diagnosis he claims to have not needed to visit the doctor for 40 years. Then one day he developed an incredibly sharp pain in his right shoulder, as if someone were "sticking a knife in me all the time", he said. After an initial diagnosis of the inflammatory lung condition pleurisy, David returned to the doctor when the pain moved from his shoulder to the base of his spine.

Following a round of tests in hospital, David was diagnosed with multiple myeloma, which he was told was incurable but treatable. He began treatment right away.

Beau's attentiveness reached new heights when David returned from hospital, as if she knew he needed extra care and she was going to do all she could to provide it. David said: "She'd lay alongside me, she'd sit alongside me, she just didn't leave me. She obviously knew that I was ill because I was always in bed and she took to sleeping up on my shoulder by my head."

Going through chemotherapy posed new challenges. David would often feel unsteady on his feet, but Beau would be there to keep an eye on him whenever needed – such as when he was showering – and she diligently kept up her night-watch duties, aware when something was not right.

David said: "She obviously sensed it so she would either put her nose against my nose and breathe on me, or her whiskers would make me wake up. Or if I didn't react to it, she would sit there and with her right paw she'd tap my face and wake me up."

In May 2022, David underwent a stem cell transplant and began a monthly medication programme. His health had greatly improved, but Beau was true to her "fluffy nurse" role and continued to stay by his side. David said: "She just follows me around like a dog, she's a brilliant little cat."

Beau was shortlisted in the National Cat Awards 2023 in recognition of her care and attentiveness in her owner's time of need.

David said: "She just gives back love and affection and I think she's brilliant. She is one in a million cats."

Did you know?

Cats are thought to be one of the few animals on the planet that cannot taste sugar. Cats have taste buds, but the receptors on their tongues responsible for detecting sweetness are not very sensitive so they have a distinct lack of a sweet tooth. Rather, cats' taste receptors are tuned in to detect meaty flavours, which is why they are carnivores.

BOB: THE STREET CAT WITH A BIG HEART

In 2007, recovering heroin addict James Bowen was struggling. After years of sleeping rough on the streets of London, in the UK, he was working as a street musician attempting to scrape a bit of money together each day and living in a one-bedroom council flat. He was taking life one step at a time, hoping something positive that could turn his life around might be just around the corner.

That's when Bob walked into his life. James came across the hungry ginger cat in the stairwell of his building and noticed he had a rather nasty wound on his leg. He pitied the cat, but felt in no fit state to help as he was struggling to make ends meet.

A couple of days later, the cat was still there. Clearly a stray, the cat needed help and James decided to take him to the RSPCA, who diagnosed an abscess and prescribed antibiotics. James spent the little money he had on medication for the cat and took him home. That's when he named him Bob.

Adopting Bob was never supposed to be a permanent arrangement. James felt he could ill afford to look after himself, let alone another creature, and assumed Bob would want to move on as soon as he was feeling better. But Bob proved to be a loyal companion to James and showed his gratitude to the musician by never wanting to leave his side.

When James returned from a day busking on the street, Bob would be waiting for him. When he left the house to head out for a day's work, Bob wanted to come too. In fact, Bob wanted to be with James all the time. It wasn't long before James felt he had no choice but to take Bob with him wherever he went. He would walk the streets of London with Bob on his shoulder and perform for the city's commuters and residents with Bob at his side.

Bob's presence really turned things around for James. People started to notice him as he sat on the street and played his music; they would even stop to talk to him and take photos of him and Bob. People were far more generous with their spare change when Bob was around and James found he was earning far more than he ever had before. This newfound wealth enabled James to get Bob microchipped and vaccinated, and he even bought him a little harness to keep him safe on the streets.

In 2008, after a few brushes with the London police for busking where he shouldn't have been, James decided to start selling *The Big Issue*, a magazine published globally and sold on the streets by homeless and long-term unemployed people. With Bob still at his side daily, the pair attracted loyal customers and something of a following on social media.

A literary agent caught sight of James and Bob online and reached out to James about writing a book. Along with a ghostwriter he put pen to paper and in 2012 *A Street Cat Named Bob* was published. The book was a roaring success and was translated into 40 different languages. Eight books followed over the years and by 2020 more than 8 million copies had been sold. Bob became a feline celebrity and regularly made public appearances. In 2013 he was awarded the Tails of the Unexpected Honour at the British Animal Honours – a prestigious event celebrating Britain's most extraordinary creatures.

James was overwhelmed and wanted to give something back. When times had been hard, the Blue Cross charity had often treated Bob with no charge and the organization was responsible for regularly saving the lives of many other animals in great need. James and Bob launched a campaign that raised more than £20,000 for the charity.

James said: "The wonderful thing about all this is I have a purpose now. I can help with the Blue Cross, with drug rehabilitation and homeless programmes. I am able to do all of this, just from my voice, just from saving one cat. It's amazing to be able to give back."

In 2016 the original book was adapted into a film and in 2020 a sequel was released. Tragically, in 2020, Bob died after being hit by a car. His legacy was something else: the effect he had on his owner's life was profound and this exceptional street cat had touched the hearts of millions of people worldwide.

Did you know?

In the wild, adult cats do not meow – this sound is reserved for kittens. The meow from our cats is thought to be a result of domestication; a way for them to get our attention. Cats have learned that their meows provoke certain responses. For example, the meow is actually a purr mixed with a high-pitched cry and, according to studies, much like a baby's cry, humans find these sounds difficult to ignore.

BRIAN: A WALK IN THE CLOUDS

In March 2023, on a JetBlue flight between Southern California and New York City, a grey-and-white cat was found wandering the aisles.

Much to the surprise of those on board, a flight attendant held the cat up for all to see and appealed to the passengers in the cabin in the hunt for the creature's owner.

Author and columnist Yi Shun Lai shared a photograph on Twitter of this incident and wrote: "On last night's @JetBlue flight, ONT-JFK: 'Is anyone missing a CAT. A grey-and-white CAT.' Yes I woke up for this."

It wasn't long before the cat's owners were located – as it turned out, the cat's name was Brian and he had somehow escaped from his carrier and gone for a stroll to explore the plane.

Yi Shun's tweet went viral, attracting more than 133,000 likes. Brian's owner Alexis also provided an update: "He's doing great! My partner and I travel with him in a cat-backpack and the bottom flap isn't very secure. So Brian must've nudged it open while we were asleep."

She added: "Thank you for all the love, he's safe and sound but definitely not sorry."

One social media user said: "Retired flight attendant here. My dream flight would have been one full of cats and dogs, no humans."

In January of the same year, a cat was found wandering about on a flight from Dallas to San Francisco. A video on social media site TikTok shows the flight attendant holding the tabby cat as if it were "a bomb" and walking up the aisle showing the creature to the passengers in an attempt to locate its owner. The owner is seen rushing down the aisle to retrieve their pet who had escaped from its carrier to cause a little chaos onboard.

One social media user commented: "Honestly, the loose cat would make my flight 10,000 x better". Another said: "Was the seatbelt light on? No, then isn't he free to move around the cabin?"

CASPER: THE COMMUTING CAT

A black-and-white mog had been living at an animal rescue centre in Weymouth, Dorset, UK, when he was adopted by Susan Finden. Susan realized quickly that he was an independent cat who liked his space and often wandered off. She decided to name him Casper after Casper the Friendly Ghost due to his propensity for disappearing.

Susan started hearing reports of Casper visiting nearby offices and businesses, crossing busy roads to get there, clearly unafraid of heavy traffic and large vehicles. Fearing for his safety, she tried to keep him indoors, but he always managed to get out.

In 2006, Susan moved to Plymouth in Dorset. She would go to work each day, leaving Casper at home and only dreaming of what he might be getting up to while she was out. It was almost three years before Susan discovered that Casper had in fact been regularly trotting up to the bus stop opposite her house. Here he would wait in line with the other passengers, before boarding a bus when it came along. Once he had located a seat, he made himself comfortable for the 11-mile journey all the way into the city centre and back to the bus stop opposite his house. The drivers quickly became accustomed to their feline passenger and knew which bus stop to let him off the bus.

Susan was moved by the actions of the bus drivers and contacted the bus company to thank them. She wrote a letter to the local newspaper to further highlight their kindness, which caught the attention of media outlets up and down the country. Soon Casper was featured on the BBC News boarding a bus and making his journey to the city. It wasn't long before his story was picked up around the world and Casper became something of a global celebrity.

The bus company decorated the side of their buses with a gigantic picture of their beloved Casper and said he could travel for free on their buses any time. PR manager Karen Baxter said: "In cat years he's an OAP so he'd get a free bus pass anyway."

Sadly, Casper was hit by a taxi in 2010 and died of his injuries. Susan received messages of condolence from all corners of the globe – Casper had touched the hearts of many with his independent spirit and travelling confidence.

Susan placed a note at the bus stop: "Many local people knew Casper, who loved everyone. He also enjoyed the bus journeys. Sadly, a motorist hit him… and did not stop. Casper died from his injuries. He will be greatly missed. He was a much-loved pet who had so much character. Thank you to all those who befriended him."

Following Casper's death, with the help of a ghostwriter Susan wrote a book called *Casper the Commuting Cat*, spreading stories of Casper's determination to explore far and wide.

CHEETO: PATRON SAINT OF LOST CATS

After helping her neighbour to successfully find her missing cat, Kat Albrecht from Seattle, Washington, USA, knew she had to help others to recover their lost pets too.

She set up the Missing Pet Partnership to help with just this. We've all seen an abundance of missing pet posters in our lifetime and Kat felt if such an organization could help the pets and their owners be reunited, perhaps there wouldn't be so many of the posters – or they at least wouldn't hang there for so long, weathering and becoming even sadder to look at.

Having spent years working as a police investigator, Kat had extensive experience working with sniffer dogs and knew this was likely the best route to recovering lost pets. With the right training, dogs and their keen sense of smell could seek out a misplaced creature with relative ease.

Kat wanted to help all pets, but was aware most of the missing animals tended to be cats. Felines especially can find themselves stuck in small spaces, holes, sheds, lofts, basements or garages, but that was where the sniffer dogs came in – they could seek out the missing cats before it was too late.

Training the dogs to sniff out a cat required a willing feline participant that could itself be quickly trained to lie still in a hiding place for the dogs to find. Up stepped Cheeto, a fearless and good-natured ginger-and-white tomcat. Luckily, he also enjoyed the company of dogs.

Cheeto's job was to climb into a black mesh bag or a crate and keep quiet and still while the dogs attempted to locate him; Cheeto was the ultimate professional and always remained silent. He would often be hidden in garden waste, woodlands or under the deck of a house. Cheeto staying quiet was essential to the dogs' training, so they relied on their smell, rather than their hearing, to locate him. Whenever the dogs found Cheeto they would be rewarded with a treat.

Cheeto was hailed by the trainers as a patient and good-natured cat, and an expert in dog training. He sadly passed away in 2014, but the Missing Pet Partnership, which is now called Mission Reunite, credited his professionalism with helping to bring back home safely more than 300 cats to their eternally grateful owners.

MRS CHIPPY: ENDURING FRIENDSHIP

Mrs Chippy was a tabby tomcat who accompanied Ernest Shackleton and his crew on their ill-fated voyage across the Antarctic aboard *Endurance*.

Endurance set sail from London's East India Docks on 1 August 1914, with 28 men on board along with 70 sledge dogs and Mrs Chippy. Curiously, Mrs Chippy came about his name because he was the companion of the ship's carpenter, Harry McNish. The tabby would follow Harry around the ship, and with "chippy" being slang for carpenter and the rest of the crew deciding the cat was behaving as if it were Harry's possessive wife, so Mrs Chippy was born.

Harry had found Mrs Chippy – then a stray – curled up in his toolbox as he was preparing to load it onto the ship. He thought a feline friend aboard would be ideal. Shackleton was also pleased to have a mouser aboard to protect food stores.

The crew liked having the sweet-natured Mrs Chippy around and he garnered much attention as he wandered about the ship. The sledge dogs chained up in kennels below deck were not huge fans of Mrs Chippy and would howl through the cage bars, no doubt frustrated at being cooped up while he roamed free.

In January 1915, *Endurance* became trapped in frozen pack ice in the Weddell Sea, some 310 miles from land. The crew worked tirelessly to free the ship from the ice, while Mrs Chippy disappeared for five days. The crew feared that he had ventured onto the ice and not made it back, but when he returned their spirits lifted.

Mrs Chippy was not a fan of the ice and spent much of his time on the marooned ship below deck, out of the cold. Months passed and still the ship was no closer to being released from the ice. Mrs Chippy slept a lot and his presence instilled a sense of calm in those aboard *Endurance*.

Years later one crew member said: "Mrs Chippy's almost total disregard for the diabolical forces at work on the ship was more than remarkable – it was inspirational. Such perfect courage is, alas, not to be found in our modern age."

By October 1915 the ship was creaking under the pressure of the ice and Shackleton decided the crew must abandon ship. There were three lifeboats on board *Endurance* and some tough decisions had to be made. Shackleton decided that the sledge dogs and Mrs Chippy had to be left behind. The crew were heartbroken – and none more so than Harry – but they were loyal to Shackleton and didn't question his authority.

Harry allegedly took Mrs Chippy to his tent to say his final farewell and gave him a bowl of sardines that he had laced with a tranquilizer – allowing the tabby some peace when the end came. Mrs Chippy ate the sardines and fell into a deep sleep. However, Shackleton's book *South* tells a different story – on 29 October the cat was shot along with some of the dogs.

It has been said since that Harry never forgave Shackleton for what happened to his beloved cat – and made no secret of it. The pair fell out and with their relationship seemingly beyond repair, Shackleton refused to recommend Harry for a Polar Medal for bravery, despite the fact that Harry's carpentry arguably ensured the lifeboats were seaworthy and no doubt saved the lives of all members of the crew.

In 1925, Harry moved to Wellington, New Zealand, but he never forgot Mrs Chippy. Baden Norris, curator of Antarctic history at the Canterbury Museum remembers meeting Harry later in his life. Norris recalled: "The only thing I remember him saying was that Shackleton shot his cat."

Harry died in 1930 with little to call his own, having laboured on the waterfront in Wellington until retirement due to age and injury. His grave in Karori Cemetery lay unmarked until 1959 when the New Zealand Antarctic Society paid for a headstone. In 2004 the society commissioned a life-size bronze statue of Mrs Chippy to adorn Harry's grave. Harry's grandson Tom was thrilled with the statue and said: "I think the cat was more important to him than the Polar Medal."

CHRISTOPHER: THE WONDER CAT

Christopher was four years old when he was involved in a road accident in San Francisco, California, USA. A group of cyclists stopped when they saw him by the side of the road, rescued him and took him to the local Redwood City veterinary clinic.

Poor Christopher was unable to stand due to a fractured pelvis, but thanks to the dedication and care of the clinic staff he was nursed back to health and recovered to walk once more.

The little cat was discovered to be a stray, but during his time in recovery at the clinic the staff realized he was actually a very special feline indeed. They even went as far as to call him a "guardian angel", "wonder cat" and "miracle kitty". But what made Christopher so remarkable?

The staff believed he possessed a kind of sixth sense and could tune in to the other cats, knowing when they needed help and support when no one else could tell.

"It's weird, it's really true that he seems to understand things," said Monica Thompson, chief veterinarian and founder of the clinic. "He knows when he can help. He alerts us when things aren't right about a cat."

The caring cat would sit outside the cages of sick moggies, meowing and asking to be let in. Staff would oblige and Christopher would head in to nuzzle and comfort the unwell residents, lying with them and offering support with his presence.

On one occasion he was instrumental in saving the life of a tiny black kitten who had arrived at the clinic with severe anaemia. The only thing that was going to save her was a blood transfusion, but no matter how hard Monica tried, she couldn't draw enough blood from the kitten to determine her blood type: she was running out of time and Monica wasn't sure what she could do next.

Christopher appeared and jumped up on the operating table. He rubbed himself up against Monica and nuzzled the kitten. At first, Monica lifted Christopher off the operating table and placed him back down on the floor, but he persisted and jumped up again, rubbing up against Monica as she stood there, at a loss as to how to save the little kitten.

She realized that perhaps Christopher was trying to tell her something – he was after all their cat with the sixth sense. Monica decided to try something. She put all her faith in the wonder cat and drew Christopher's blood to use it for the transfusion to try and save the poorly little kitten.

Unbeknown to Monica, the kitten had a reasonably rare blood type, B, which occurs in around 25 per cent of the cat population – usually purebreds. Almost unbelievably, Christopher was also type B. Monica took the chance and transfused his blood to the kitten and its life was saved. In a matter of hours, the tiny fluffball was back on her feet as if nothing had even happened. Monica said: "If I hadn't paid attention to Christopher, I probably would have lost the cat."

Christopher also became known around the clinic as the "feral kitten tamer" after being let into a cage with two stray kittens who would growl and hiss at anyone who would come close. Over the next couple of weeks, Christopher taught the kittens all they needed to know about being a cat. He tamed the once untouchable kittens and they adored him – when he left the cage they would cry for him to come back. Both were rescued to forever homes thanks to his caring and nurturing nature.

Despite many requests to adopt Christopher, the clinic preferred to keep their secret weapon close and Christopher the wonder cat continued to provide comfort for the sick and education for the feral cats that were brought to the clinic. He also continued to act as a blood donor. A truly remarkable cat.

COCO: SQUIRREL SAVIOUR

When Decan Andersen rescued a baby squirrel outside his apartment building in Denmark, he assumed he would be the one to care for it and nurture it back to health, so you can imagine his surprise when his cat Coco stepped up to the task instead.

Decan discovered the injured red squirrel one day after it had fallen from the roof four storeys up and hit a tree branch on the way down, injuring its chest. Decan guessed the tiny creature couldn't have been more than about five weeks old and in its injured state it had been abandoned by its family.

Decan scooped up the squirrel and took it into his apartment. His family and ginger cat Coco welcomed the new arrival, whom they named Tintin. Coco had a brother, Tiger the black-and-white cat, and Decan had adopted the pair four years earlier from a family who were unable to care for them. The two cats were quite different from each other – Decan knew Coco would be a friend to Tintin and when he placed the tiny squirrel next to her she knew what to do, proceeding to clean him and keep him warm.

Decan said on Instagram: "Tiger has always been the badass of the two, while Coco was the loving, caring and cuddly little princess. When Tiger would come home with a mouse or bird, Coco would fight her brother for it; she would take it from him and care for it, licking it, warming it like it was her own little kitten. Time went on and then four years later a miracle landed in our garden. Tintin had arrived. I knew Coco so had no worries in my heart when I handed her the wounded squirrel baby."

Little Tintin made a full recovery and was granted special permission to remain with the family. While it's illegal in Denmark to keep wild animals as pets, Tintin was so accustomed to humans by this point that it would have been dangerous to release him back into the wild, and so allowances were made. Squirrels can live for up to 20 years and Tintin's new family wanted to spend that time with him. The family even fashioned him some jumpers out of old socks and he fitted right in with daily life with them all, growing especially close to Coco, who continued to treat him as if he were her own offspring.

Sadly, one year after Tintin joined the family, Coco died. The family were overjoyed when Tiger stepped into her shoes and began to care for the little squirrel in the way his sister once had.

Decan said: "Tintin and Tiger bonded on a whole new level. They always greet each other with nose bumps. I have lost count of how many times Tiger has spotted and chased off hawks, other cats and, yes, even a dog to protect Tintin."

Tintin is something of a social media superstar, with almost 120,000 followers on Instagram, and has appeared in newspapers and magazines across the world – but he wouldn't be here without the care and love of his beloved cat-mother, Coco.

COLIN'S: THE PORT CAT

Around 1991, a tiny calico kitten was found alone in a tanker terminal in New Plymouth, New Zealand, and was rescued by manager Colin Butler. She was so small that Colin carried her around in his pocket for the best part of a fortnight to keep her safe.

Colin named the tiny kitten Queenie. When he retired to Australia he was forced to leave her behind. She stuck around – after all, the tanker terminal was her home – and she became known to staff as "Colin's Cat" or simply "Colin's".

Terminal superintendent Gordon Macpherson became responsible for Colin's and she took on duties around the terminal, chasing away feral cats and dogs, and guarding her territory. She got wise to staff shift patterns, making sure to beg for food *before* workers went off shift and, when she desired second helpings, approaching the incoming workers as they were beginning their stint.

In 2001, Colin's strolled aboard a methanol tanker and encountered crew member Jeong Yun-Seok. Jeong took her off to find something to eat. After their meal, the pair fell asleep in Jeong's cabin and when they awoke the tanker had already left port. Its destination? South Korea!

Colin's had often wandered onto New Zealand tankers but she had never left the port, so was not used to life on the water. She was seasick at first, but soon found all four of her sea legs and settled in for the long journey.

The tanker's captain Chang Seong-Mo emailed photos of Colin's back to the port to assure everybody she was safe and well. She spent much of her time on the voyage sleeping on Jeong's sofa and existed on a diet of "salmon, beef and snacks".

Now that the port staff knew Colin's was alive and well, they hatched a plan that would involve Gordon flying to South Korea and meeting Colin's from the ship as it docked. He would then fly back to New Plymouth with the globe-trotting mog.

By this point Colin's was grabbing headlines all over the world. Cat food brands battled it out to sponsor her trip back home and, with the help of Korean Airlines, Gordon arrived in the tanker's destination port of Yeosu before the ship docked and waited patiently for his cat's arrival. There was much in the way of paperwork to negotiate as Colin's should have been quarantined on arrival. After the situation was explained, the authorities agreed to allow Colin's to slope off the ship and into Gordon's arms. She was transported in a sealed carrier and taken straight to Seoul Airport to catch a flight back to New Zealand.

Gordon said: "She purred a lot and seemed pleased to see me. I'll have to give her a talking to and tell her not to speak to strange men in the future."

Jeong had apparently grown close to Colin's on the journey to South Korea and was said to have "spoiled her rotten". He was going to miss her a great deal.

New Zealand authorities issued a special permit for Colin's, allowing her to bypass quarantine and she was greeted at the airport by a white limousine and multiple TV cameras. The port staff laid on a welcome home party, which was attended by the mayor. Colin's was awarded Honorary Ambassador of the District in recognition of her "international relations" by New Plymouth District Council.

A few years later the port published an update on Colin's exploits, claiming she was living a far quieter life – her seafaring days were over. Since her adventure, she had not set foot on a tanker at the port, but still liked to hunt seagulls. Following the media attention, her original owner Colin Butler had also stopped by to visit the cat he rescued as a tiny kitten.

In 2007, Colin's passed away after a long life. She was buried in the port grounds and a plaque was installed in her memory. She is still remembered for her remarkable life and journey, and visitors often stop by the port to see the plaque and the place she called home for so many years.

DALI: A TALE OF SURVIVAL

Dali was a remarkable cat who survived for four weeks marooned in the middle of a river.

When the four-year-old black-and-white cat went missing, owners Rebecca Wilson and Ryan Benson from northern England, were distraught. They spent weeks searching for their beloved feline friend but Dali had seemingly vanished without a trace. Her owners were starting to give up hope when someone discovered the little cat at the foot of a 15 foot drop into Bradford Beck.

Dali was spotted clinging to a square patch of rocks in the middle of the river. The person who discovered her noticed how bedraggled and distressed she looked. Her owners suspected she had been stranded, surrounded by the flowing water, ever since she had vanished. She was found to be malnourished, hungry and exhausted, and her claws needed attention as she had splintered them while presumably making multiple attempts to desperately scale the wall to safety.

According to Rebecca: "We'd searched everywhere, put up posters and lots of posts on social media, but she was nowhere to be found. We were both really upset and my partner had started to give up hope, but I had a feeling she was out there somewhere."

Ryan borrowed some waders and headed into the water to save Dali. The little cat was overjoyed to see him and, quite unusually for her, bounded into her cat carrier.

One trip to the vets later, Dali was sent home with clipped claws and instructions to be fed extra portions after her misadventure on the water.

Rebecca said: "We're incredibly lucky that there hadn't been much rainfall, because if the beck had risen then she would have been swept away by the current. She's a very lucky and brave cat and we were absolutely overjoyed to have her home. We've no idea how she got down there but fortunately she seems to avoid going near that area now."

Dali was shortlisted for the National Cat Awards 2023 – the feline Oscars, if you will – for her bravery in the face of the challenge to survive the beck.

Awards organizer Ashley Fryer hailed Dali's efforts: "Dali's story is an amazing tale of bravery and determination to survive, and we're thrilled it had a happy ending. Thanks to Rebecca and Ryan's tireless efforts to find her, they were quickly alerted when she was finally spotted and Ryan was able to rescue her. It's safe to say that Dali has definitely used up one of her nine lives, but her tale is a lovely story of a community working together."

DELLA: THE DUCK WHISPERER

A stray farm cat living in County Offaly, Ireland, turned out to be the most loving adoptive mother to a completely different species living in the vicinity.

Emma and Ronan Lally lived and worked on the farm and had a large collection of animals; what they didn't have were ducks. They were keen to rectify this, so they bought some fertilized eggs, stored them in the safety of the barn and eagerly waited for them to hatch.

The pair made regular checks on the unhatched eggs and one morning Ronan discovered eggshells in the nest. The ducklings had hatched but were nowhere to be seen. Ronan scoured the barn, but couldn't find the ducklings anywhere. Just then, a cat leaped out of the hayloft and took him by surprise. He had never seen the cat before, but grew nervous at the thought of her being around the tiny new ducklings – knowing only too well they could quickly become feline prey.

Emma and Ronan searched high and low around the farm for any sign of the ducklings, eventually encountering the cat again. Their hearts sank when they saw she was holding one of the tiny yellow creatures in her mouth, until they realized the tenderness with which she was doing so. The cat was carrying the duckling as if it were her kitten. They followed her inside and she led them to a nest of her own, where the other two ducklings were sitting. She carefully dropped the tiny duckling from her mouth into the nest and snuggled down next to the little birds. The ducklings nestled into the cat and she put her paw around them in a protective gesture.

Ronan and Emma were both amazed at the affectionate display they were witnessing. They decided then and there to name the cat who had come to call their farm home – they settled on Della.

Emma said: "She was very content. She was purring and was really loving toward the ducklings."

As Emma carefully approached Della to pet her, she noticed to her astonishment three tiny kittens in the nest behind her. Della had obviously given birth to these three adorable fluffballs very recently and her mothering instinct was so strong that when she saw the brand new ducks without a parent it felt natural to assume that role and care for them.

Della continued to care for the ducklings and, incredibly, even nursed them while they were little. The ducks grew quickly and before too long flew the nest and went to live on the pond that had always been their intended home. Emma and Ronan adopted Della and her kittens and loved having the cat family roaming around their farm.

Did you know?

Many other cats have adopted outside their species too. In Brazil there were reports of a woman discovering her cat had given birth to a litter of kittens *and* a litter of puppies! Of course, it turned out the cat had encountered the abandoned litter of puppies while she was in mothering mode and had taken it upon herself to foster them.

DEWEY: THE LIBRARY CAT

In small-town Iowa, USA, one cold January night in 1988, an unexpected visitor tumbled into the Spencer local library via the book-return chute. The next morning, library staff discovered a little ginger cat by following the sound of whimpering.

It had been a freezing night so the staff warmed the feline intruder up and gave him some milk. He purred the whole time they were paying attention to him and the appreciation was mutual. Library staff decided they would like to keep him – a library cat sounded like a good idea. An appropriate name was in order: Dewey (after the Dewey decimal system used to catalogue library books) or, to give him his full title, Dewey Readmore Books.

Dewey was neutered and vaccinated and settled right in at the library. Not only was he beloved by all staff, but the residents of Spencer came to adore him too. News of his arrival down the book chute carried and those from further afield came to visit him, as well as send donations for his food and care.

He would greet people at the front desk of the library as they arrived to peruse the books and never missed a library meeting. He was an incredibly sociable cat and disliked it when the library was closed.

Library director Vicki Myron took responsibility for Dewey's care and said the cat used to wave at her as she approached the library in the mornings.

Dewey became something of a celebrity cat across America and brought a great deal of publicity to the small-town library. He featured in national magazines, books, on TV and had his own postcards. He was even the star of a documentary about library cats up and down the country: *Puss in Books: Adventures of the Library Cat*. The height of his fame saw him starring as the January cat on a calendar sold nationwide.

As Dewey reached old age, his health began to fail and he slept a lot more. Despite a long list of ailments, the library cat was true to his duties and continued to patrol his workplace and greet all who browsed the shelves. Visitors were asked to only pet him on the head and shoulders, and not to pick him up, due to his arthritis, but he never lost his charm. Library staff reported that in his old age he began to reject cat food and developed a peculiar taste for cheeseburgers and beef sandwiches!

Dewey sadly passed away shortly after his 19th birthday after being diagnosed with a stomach tumour on top of a long list of other ailments. As he began to deteriorate, Vicki knew the kindest thing to do was to put him to sleep. She said: "I called all the staff and they came out to say goodbye. It was one of the most difficult things I have ever done, but I knew I had to do it because he was suffering and I'd never let him be in pain."

Hundreds of newspapers up and down the country ran an obituary in tribute to the dedicated library cat and Dewey was cremated and buried in front of his beloved workplace. A memorial stone marks the burial spot, which reads: "In loving memory of Dewey Readmore Books. World-famous library cat." Dewey was also memorialized in bronze sculpture form by Heather Beary, who created a sculpted image of the cat perched atop an open book, with his name underneath.

In 2008, Dewey also became the subject of a book written by Vicki along with Bret Witter, which was published all over the world. *Dewey: The Small Town Library Cat Who Touched the World* sold more than a million copies in the year after it was published and topped *The New York Times* bestsellers list for several weeks straight.

And if you ever find yourself in East Leach Park in Spencer, Iowa, take a good look at the monument that stands there. Among the mosaic depictions you will find a little ginger cat leafing through a library book – now who that could be?

DONALD: A FRIEND TO ALL

Tobias Paul and his partner lived in Sackville, New Brunswick, Canada. They decided to adopt a cat from the SPCA and brought home a black long-haired feline named Donald. It wasn't long before they realized Donald was incredibly friendly to everyone he came into contact with – and that meant *everyone*.

Donald was always keen to leave the house with his owners, so Paul started taking him for walks around the neighbourhood and he would follow him as a dog would. Paul said: "Donald doesn't just follow us around, he will follow anyone he finds, and he'll follow them home and try to go inside their house."

Living in downtown Sackville, which has a university community as well as many businesses, Donald's behaviour was starting to get noticed by the local residents he used to tag along with. Many people presumed he must be a stray looking for food and shelter, and various posts online alluded to this, with locals concerned that he might need rehoming.

One local resident, Jean-Paul Lavoie, set up a Facebook group for people to record their sightings of Donald. He said: "It became a sort of sensation after a few weeks. Within 24 hours we had 250 members and now we're at almost 800 members."

The local community's fixation on this friendly local cat was as bizarre as it was charming, with many putting it down to "pandemic" fatigue (this happening in summer

2021) and the culture wars dividing online communities. It was time for something more light-hearted to focus on.

One member of the group said: "Donald is an actual cat, yes, but doesn't he represent more? A sense of freedom; of community; an openness and boldness; the assumption that everyone is a friend and everywhere is home."

Lavoie was a regular at a microbrewery in town that had also taken an interest in Donald as he was a regular visitor to the brewery and tap room. The Bagtown Brewing Company pledged to release a beer dedicated to Donald if the Facebook group's member community surpassed 500 people. What started as something of a joke quickly became a shrewd business move, as Bagtown owner Anthony Maddalena rose to the challenge and brewed a milk stout in homage to the wandering friendly cat.

The limited release – "Donald: A Sackville Cat" – featured a photograph of Donald on a dark-coloured label, with his name across a scroll and the description reading "soft and approachable milk stout". The brew was hugely popular and sold out in a matter of days.

While Paul remained somewhat baffled by all the attention, he admitted he was pleased that local residents no longer regarded Donald as a stray and knew he was a well-looked-after cat who simply had a sociable, independent spirit and curiosity like no other.

DUCHESS: A NOSE FOR DANGER

Tess Guthrie lived in New South Wales, Australia, with her two-year-old daughter Zara and cat Duchess. One day Duchess started hissing, stopped eating her food and was strangely skittish. All of this was very unusual for Duchess – a usually healthy and well-rounded feline.

The odd behaviour continued for several days. Duchess was usually such a happy, gentle cat. Tess made an appointment at the vets for the next day in the hope they could tell her what could be distressing her pet. That evening she left some food out for Duchess, hoping she would eat at least a bit of it, and put Zara to bed.

Tess went to bed herself, but was woken up a few hours later by Duchess hissing loudly. Tess put the light on to see what was causing her such agitation. To her dismay, she saw a huge python coiled around Zara's arm.

Tess couldn't believe it. She said: "At the same time I was freaking out at what I was seeing, I realized what the cat had been carrying on about for days."

The snake was wrapped around her daughter's arm three times and had a powerful grip, but naturally Tess had to do something. Having grown up in Australia, where snakes are common, she knew what to do in this situation but it was still a big challenge.

Tess said: "I grabbed the snake's head to pry it off. I think it was startled, so it started to really bite into Zara's hand. It was wrapped around her arm three or four times and so it had a really good grip. I couldn't stop wondering how long it had been under my bed."

Tess managed to unwind the snake from her daughter and throw it across the room. The pair then ran out of the house and headed to hospital.

Both Tess and Zara were treated for snake bites, and each made a full recovery. The python was retrieved from the house the next day by a professional snake handler, who took it far away and released it back into the wild.

The expert suggested the python had viewed Tess and Zara as a source of warmth. It was Duchess who had saved her family, clearly spying the snake and sensing the danger several days before it showed itself. Had she not woken Tess that night, who knows what might have happened.

DUSJA: AN UNLIKELY FRIENDSHIP

In 2007 at St Petersburg Zoo in Russia, an unlikely relationship developed between a feline pair. Staff were doing the rounds and checking on the animals, when a tiny calico kitten was spotted in the enclosure housing Linda the young European lynx. The staff recognized her as a young stray who had taken to wandering around the zoo in search of food and shelter and they suspected she may have thought Linda was her mother. At first the staff were concerned for the safety of the kitten – as lynx cats can be vicious predators – and were worried Linda might attack the young cat. As it turned out, they had nothing to worry about.

Linda had been quite charmed by her little friend and the two were perfectly at ease with one another. Still a juvenile lynx, Linda was not yet fully grown, although an adult of the species can grow up to four times the size of a domestic cat – up to 51 inches in length and weighing up to 21 kilograms. So eventually, Linda could come to tower over the kitten!

The kitten didn't appear to be going anywhere, so she was adopted by the zoo and named Dusja: "darling" in Russian. Dusja settled in and her and Linda were inseparable. They grew up side by side, grooming each other and sleeping curled up as one. Linda grew to be much larger than her dear little friend, but she remained ever gentle with the kitten. The bond that developed between the two was long-lasting and was documented all over the world, delighting animal lovers in all corners of the globe.

Other unlikely friendships forged between cats and other animals include Leonardo diCatzio, who became very close pals with Mortiz the pig and would cuddle up to him for a nap, stroke him and purr loudly; Della the farm cat who raised three ducklings; GG the kitten who struck up a friendship with several goats and even began mimicking them; British shorthair Ponzu and Mango the sun conure parrot lived together and were the best of friends; and George, the 60-kilogram mastiff, couldn't be separated from abandoned kitten Wendy when she came to live with his family.

DYMKA: THE BIONIC CAT

When little grey cat Dymka lost her paws to frostbite she was determined to keep on going – and thankfully there were enough supportive humans around her who enabled that determination.

Dymka, which means "mist" in Russian, lost her paws to frostbite in the Siberian city of Novokuznetsk in Russia. It was not known whether Dymka was a stray or had been abandoned by her previous owner, but she was found by the side of the road and brought into her local veterinary clinic by a local resident. The staff presumed the cat had either run away and got lost, or had fallen out of a window.

With the average winter temperatures in Siberia around -25°C (-13°F), veterinarian Sergei Gorshkov said: "Unfortunately, frostbite in animals is a very real problem in Siberia."

The clinic had two options – to either put her to sleep permanently or save her. Sergei wanted to fight for Dymka so she underwent surgery to have all four of her paws amputated, along with both of her ears and part of her tail.

Instead of leaving her pawless, the clinic then joined forces with researchers from Tomsk Polytechnic University to create a set of 3D-printed prosthetics for Dymka. These were installed into her body via titanium implants fused to her leg bones. The front legs were attached in July 2019, followed by the hind legs in December of the same year to complete the transition.

Following her surgery, Dymka was rehomed with the local woman who had originally found her by the side of the road. A happy ending for all.

ERIC: CAT INFLUENCER EXTRAORDINAIRE

Eric had a tough start in life, but with some love, care and a lot of determination, he pulled through and rose to be a social star.

The pint-sized ginger kitten was rescued from the streets by Strictly Strays, a charity in Tyne and Wear, UK. With numerous issues to battle, including cat flu, which made him very poorly and had a lasting impact on his health, Eric had much to contend with from the off. He was given food and medicine, and was slowly nursed back to health by the charity.

Paul Richardson and Helen Aitchinson spotted Eric on Facebook in May 2020 in a post calling on cat lovers to offer him a forever home. They fell for the four-year-old cat immediately and brought him home to live with them in nearby Hadrian Park. After the death of their beloved cat Holly eight years before, the pair had decided they would not get another cat, but smiling Eric stole their hearts when they spotted him that day. According to Paul: "We wanted to offer a cat a home and really wanted to give him a chance at life – he is a lush little cat with small legs but a big heart."

The pair realized quickly that Eric was a very photogenic cat who liked to pose for photos and videos: he even seemed to be "smiling" in each one. Cottoning on to the popularity of other pet accounts on social media, Paul and Helen decided to set Eric up with a few of his own and started posting regularly on his behalf.

His Twitter account picked up 500 followers overnight and now stands at more than 8,400 followers, while on Instagram he has more than 4,500 and TikTok around 1,400. Paul said: "Since then it has been a bit of a media frenzy for him but he is doing really well, which is all we want for him."

Eric's social media influencer status was recognized at the National Cat Awards in 2023, when he scooped the Social Star accolade.

Paul added: "When I looked at last year's awards, I knew this was something I wanted to be a part of. Reading their stories was just amazing and seeing a cat go from being a stray or mistreated and seeing them get their happy ending is what we wanted to show."

FAITH: STRENGTH IN CONVICTION

Back in 1940, a stray-turned-church cat used her intuition to protect herself and her kitten from an air raid during the London Blitz.

St Augustine's was an Anglican church in the City of London, UK, located on Watling Street just to the east of St Paul's Cathedral. The rector at the church was one Henry Ross, who had a soft spot for felines and so when a little tabby paid them a visit, Henry was more welcoming than the verger had been.

Henry took pity on her and started to give her scraps of food, eventually letting her stay in the church; when no one claimed her, he welcomed her in permanently and named her Faith.

Faith became very popular with the church congregation and would lie on the front pew or at Henry's feet during sermons. Parishioners were always eager to say hello to Faith and give her a stroke on the way into a service if she was wandering around the churchyard.

In August 1940, she gave birth to a black-and-white tom kitten, whom Henry named Panda. Faith really took to motherhood and the pair settled in happily to their new life together in Henry's living quarters at the church.

Not long after Panda's arrival, Henry noticed Faith had begun to act weirdly – she appeared restless and was always exploring and sniffing around the different rooms. One day she came up from the basement, retrieved Panda by the scruff of his neck and headed back down there. Henry found the pair in the damp basement and brought them back upstairs to keep mother and kitten warm.

The next day, Henry realized Faith had moved the kitten down to the basement again. He duly encouraged them both back upstairs. After the trio had carried out this charade multiple times, Henry gave in and moved Faith's basket down to the basement so the pair could be comfortable in her chosen spot. Faith and Panda were content below ground and settled in among the church ephemera next to a stack of music sheets.

In the UK the period of World War Two between 7 September 1940 and 11 May 1941 became known as the Blitz: a night-time bombing campaign that relentlessly attacked the nation's industrial cities, and over the course of eight months killed 43,000 civilians – with almost half of the casualties in London.

On 9 September 1940, Henry was away from the church during the day on business and made his way home in the evening to the sound of an air-raid siren. He found a local air-raid shelter and spent the night there. The Blitz had not long begun, but the attack on London that day was particularly severe overnight. Many buildings throughout the capital were destroyed, including eight churches. Henry returned home to find only the tower of St Augustine's still standing and his home reduced to rubble.

Fire fighters asked him to step away from the scene, assuring him that no one could have survived such an aggressive bomb attack. With a heavy heart Henry thought of his beloved cats, but he did not give up hope. He approached the debris and heard a faint meowing sound emanating from a pile of timber and rubble. Henry used all his strength to move the debris and was overjoyed to see two pairs of shining eyes staring up at him. The cats were frightened and dirty, but they were unharmed.

Henry was so grateful his much-loved pets had survived and took them into the still-standing vestry to clean them up, and give them food, water and cuddles.

Faith became something of a celebrity across London when her story was reported in the papers. Messages of love and support poured in and many called for Faith to be awarded a medal for bravery. She was not eligible for the PDSA Dickin Medal as she was not a military animal, but Maria Dickin – who had founded the award – honoured Faith with her own silver medal to recognize her persistence and courage in her quest to protect her young.

FELIX AND BOLT: THE RAILWAY CATS

Two beloved cats, credited with superior pest control and winning the hearts of all who pass through, reside at the transport hub of Huddersfield railway station in West Yorkshire in the UK. Felix and Bolt can be spotted peering out of ticket office windows, patrolling platforms and taking well-earned breaks on station benches, enjoying the wealth of attention from besotted train passengers.

Felix came to live at Huddersfield station in 2011 at the tender age of nine weeks. The long-haired tuxedo cat was soon discovered to be female, but the name Felix suited her down to the ground so it stuck. It wasn't long before Felix had amassed a legion of fans and in 2015 she became something of a global celebrity when commuter Mark Allan created a Facebook page just for her.

In 2016, after five years of service, Felix was promoted to senior pest controller, which can be seen on the name badge pinned to her high-vis yellow vest – you just can't miss her as she patrols the platforms. Following the introduction of new ticket barriers, a custom-made cat flap was installed to enable Felix to pass through the barriers unaided and get on with her vital work around the station.

In 2017 writer Kate Moore immortalized Felix in her book, *Felix: The Railway Cat*. In order to research and write the book, Moore tagged along on night shifts at the station to watch Felix in action and interviewed several members of station staff. The book became a *Sunday Times* bestseller and all proceeds went to the charity Prostate Cancer UK.

In 2018, station staff decided Felix could do with a companion and black cat Bolt was introduced at Huddersfield to help out with important mousing and pigeon-chasing business. As junior pest controller Bolt is just as beloved as Felix and between them they boast a whopping 162,000 followers on their (now joint) Facebook page. The page is updated daily with photos and videos of the pair in and around the station, as well as footage of their grooming and playtime sessions.

Following the success of her book and the introduction of Bolt to Huddersfield station, Moore wrote her follow-up in 2019, *Full Steam Ahead: Adventures of a famous station cat and her kitten apprentice*.

While something of a novelty, Felix and Bolt are not the only cats to have been in residence at a railway station. Often home to a number of rodents, several stations caught on to the fact that a feline presence could be just the ticket to control the pests. Tizer, a rescue cat adopted by the British Transport Police, called King's Cross station in London his home for two years and was made an honorary constable for his services to mouse detecting. Tama, a resident cat at a railway station in western Japan, was also much loved and drew huge numbers of tourists to the station just to see her. She was named "Super Stationmaster", credited with reviving the failing railway company's fortunes and her funeral was attended by thousands of well-wishers.

FLUFFY: THE FROZEN CAT

In the winter of 2019, a long-haired grey-and-white cat from Montana, USA, used up one of its nine lives.

Fluffy lived in the city of Kalispell in the far north-west of the state, not far from the Canadian border. In January that year the region had experienced heavy snowfall amounting to around 15 inches and the temperature was a chilly -13°C (-9 °F).

On 31 January, Fluffy's owners found her frozen in a snowbank, unresponsive and with her fur matted with snow and ice. Distraught, they took her to the local animal clinic where staff immediately set to work trying to thaw her out. When Fluffy first arrived, her temperature was so low it didn't even register on the vet's thermometer.

Staff at the clinic used warm water and blankets in an attempt to warm Fluffy up, but after two hours of trying their best her temperature was still too low. She was eventually taken to the emergency room.

After a few more hours in the emergency room and all the warmth the clinic could muster, Fluffy began to show some signs of recovery. A few days later she was well enough to return home and was reunited with her family, having made a full and miraculous recovery.

The clinic posted the remarkable story of Fluffy and her incredible revival on Facebook, declaring "Fluffy is amazing!" and racking up thousands of likes, shares and comments.

FRED: UNDERCOVER CAT

Fred was a stray kitten, taken in by an animal shelter in New York City, with an important role ahead of him – he just didn't know it yet.

At just a couple of months old, the black-striped tabby was adopted along with his brother by the Brooklyn Assistant District Attorney, Carol Moran. Poor Fred was suffering with serious pneumonia and had a collapsed lung, but following a course of antibiotics, steam inhalation and a multitude of chest rubs, the little mite was on the mend and fighting fit in no time – even chasing Carol's other cats and dogs around her house.

Due to his rocky start in life and his lung condition, Carol decided to call the little ones Fred and George Wheezy – an amusing take on the mischievous twins Fred and George Weasley from the Harry Potter books and movies.

At the time, the Brooklyn district attorney's office was investigating a man suspected of posing as a veterinarian without a licence or training in animal medicine. This was a criminal offence and the poseur was a danger to animals and pets all over Brooklyn. The investigation into the Brooklyn resident – Steven Vassall – was gathering pace, but needed something more to seal the case and prosecute the fraudulent individual. The district attorney's office needed to catch him in the act. This was where Fred came in.

The kitty was given a mission: to catch the fake veterinarian in the act and save the animals of Brooklyn from potential harm in the process. It was a tough mission, but Fred Wheezy was up to the job. He went undercover to expose Vassall, posing as a patient and pretending to be the cat of undercover detective Stephanie Green-Jones.

Stephanie called the charlatan to her apartment – which had been rigged with hidden cameras – and told him Fred needed to be neutered. He told her he could perform the minor operation for $135 and was then arrested as he left the apartment with the cash in his pocket and Fred in a box.

Vassall was accused of performing medical procedures on at least 14 animals and charged with criminal mischief, unauthorized veterinary practice, injuring animals and petty larceny. He was sentenced to probation and ordered to attend a mandatory mental health programme, all the while refraining from nursing or animal care.

Fred was hailed an undercover hero and decorated with a Law Enforcement Appreciation Award by Brooklyn District Attorney, Charles J. Hynes. He was later presented with the Mayor's Alliance Award, which is reserved for truly remarkable animals.

Recognized as the first "undercover cat", Fred was inundated with offers from animal talent agencies desperate to represent him. He was even asked to appear in TV commercials. He was trained as a therapy animal and enlisted to the district attorney's office's Legal Lives programme, with the plan to take him into classrooms where he would help a handler teach children how best to treat and care for animals.

Fred settled into life as a house cat with Carol, his brother George and Carol's other cats and dogs. He was a sweet cat to his owners, but regularly chased the other animals around their home and out into the yard.

Tragically, only three months after the sting operation, Fred was at home when he escaped from the backyard and ran out into the street. He was hit by a car and died instantly. Young Fred was just 15 months old and no doubt had much more to give, but the city and its animals never forgot the first undercover cat who had helped to keep them safe.

GARY: THE ADVENTURER

In 2015 James Eastham adopted his long-haired grey-and-white cat Gary as a kitten with a broken hip from the Calgary Humane Society. Living in Canada, James is quite the adventurer. He knew he wanted a pet who could potentially accompany him on his adventures. James said: "He is normally a fairly relaxed cat, which definitely helped, but there was for sure a lot of training to get him to where he is now. Now he hikes and he paddles and he skis. He's a great little adventure buddy."

Gary and James are inseparable and wherever James goes, Gary is right there beside him. Gary's penchant for ski travel happened quite by accident. One winter, the pair had been snowed in and the only way to get around had been with a pair of skis. These days, Gary sits on James' shoulder and even has his own UV goggles.

James said: "That is his favourite way to travel when we hike. We only tried skiing after I was very confident in his ability to balance up there."

Gary has a strong social media presence and an army of followers and fans. With more than 530,000 followers on Instagram and the same number again on TikTok, it can be hard for the pair to do their adventuring these days without getting noticed.

After the pair hit the headlines in 2021, James put the public's fascination down to pandemic fatigue and people looking for something light-hearted to focus on; he had set up Gary's social media accounts in order to bring a bit of fun and joy into people's lives at a bleak and uncertain time, but little did he know the impact Gary would have on the social media communities: "Lots of people when we meet them out on the trails get really excited to see him and it's got difficult to ski even because people want to stop you to take a photo or say hi. But I think it's great, especially when things are a little bit depressing everywhere to be able to have that escape."

James did, however, issue a few words of warning about adventuring with your pet cat: "Don't just rush out, stuff Fluffy in a bag and hit the slopes," he said. "It took us a long time to work up to a point where I was comfortable skiing [with Gary] and Gary was comfortable skiing with me. We've been out hiking now for about three years together, so there's a lot of trust between us."

According to James, patience has been key and you should allow your cat to adjust to these new situations. "It's not the same as training a dog," he said. "Cats are different. They're absolutely able to adapt. They just need a bit of time and to go at their own pace."

He continued: "While there are not a lot of skiing cats, lots of people take their cats out hiking. I think it's becoming more common as people see what's possible. They have cats and want to bring them travelling with them."

GINGABURGER: THE SMOKE DETECTOR

Gingaburger was a regular visitor to Leslie's house in Hawke's Bay, New Zealand, and would often pad his paw against her bedroom window, asking to be let in so he could sleep on her bed. The large long-haired ginger feline – named for his colouring and big belly – belonged to Leslie's cousin who lived across the road.

Early one morning, Leslie was woken up by a scratching sound at the front door. She suspected it was Gingaburger, but this behaviour was unusual for him and not the way he generally liked to gain entry to her house. Leslie remembered her front door had recently been painted and rushed to find out what was going on outside.

As soon as Leslie opened the door, Gingaburger shot inside the house and headed straight for the living room – more unusual behaviour, thought Leslie, as he was usually only interested in curling up on her bed and slumbering there for hours at a time.

Gingaburger sat himself next to the cupboard that contained the water heater and started meowing very loudly while staring at the top of the door. Leslie couldn't work out what was the matter, but the ginger cat continued to meow in the direction of the cupboard.

Having had her sleep disturbed, Leslie was tired and keen to get back to sleep. She managed to coax Gingaburger, who was still meowing, out of the living room and back to her bedroom. She climbed back into bed and tried to encourage Gingaburger to do the same.

As she was settling down, Leslie heard a fluttering, crackling sound coming from the corner of the room – this side of her bedroom shared a wall with the water heater cupboard. Leslie went back to the living room and, standing on a chair, she tried to catch a glimpse of whatever was making the noise through the gap at the top of the cupboard door. She was fully expecting to see a rat and had steeled herself for the sight, when she saw the glowing embers of a fire that had started on top of her water heater.

Leslie's house was fitted with smoke alarms, but the fire had not yet set them off. How had Gingaburger smelled the smoke before the smoke alarms? Leslie immediately called the fire service who arrived promptly to put out the fire. She was hugely grateful to the clever cat for warning her and helping her to escape the fire and its toxic fumes.

Leslie said: "If I had woken up any later, I might not be here. Gingaburger is a lovely cat and a bit of a rogue. If he was a man, I would marry him."

Did you know?

Thanks to their ability to swivel their ears up to 180 degrees, cats can hear ultrasonic noises – far beyond the range of the human ear – allowing them to pinpoint sounds. Cats have 32 muscles in their outer ear to help them with the swivelling, whereas humans only have six.

HENRY IX: TITLE FIT FOR A KING

Henry could not be a more apt name for a cat living at Hampton Court Palace in Surrey, in the UK – after all, this was the most famous residence of Henry VIII – the controversial King of England who had six wives and executed two of them.

Henry IX – see what they did there? – is a black-and-white cat who strolls through the palace gardens, keeping an eye out for mice and other small pests, and doing his best to live up to his regal title.

The little furry monarch has been sleeping in the potting shed for the past eight years and day to day he keeps palace gardener Jo Ward company. The garden staff at Hampton Court regularly post photos of their royal feline on Instagram via his own account @the_hampton_court_palace_cat – especially when he makes them laugh, as he so often does. He is also a stellar companion to the night patrol staff who love having Henry IX around.

In 2023 Henry's services to royal residences were recognized when he was pronounced the winner in the Cat Colleagues category at the National Cat Awards. Gardener Jo said: "Hampton Court Palace has a long history of having a resident cat in the gardens, and since Henry came to join us eight years ago, he's become a pivotal member of the team, whether it's keeping us company while we're working, or keeping rodents at bay. Gardening can be a lonely job – and was especially during the pandemic – but Henry was always around."

HUGO: THE GOOD NEIGHBOUR

Andrew Williams lived in Berkshire, UK, with his wife Sarah. The pair didn't have a cat of their own, but were big fans of the neighbour's cats, brothers Hugo and Harvey, and always let them wander in to say hello.

Andrew worked as an engineer and had recently been carrying out some work on their bungalow. One weekend, Andrew was at home on his own as Sarah was away visiting family. He awoke at 2 a.m. with a weight on his chest and something scratching at his face. This was an unfamiliar sensation – the neighbouring cats had never been in his bedroom before.

Andrew opened his eyes to see two big eyes looking down at him: they belonged to Hugo, who had sped through the cat-flap downstairs to warn him that his house was on fire. The smoke detector didn't go off until Andrew was awake and out of bed. (He had moved it to a different spot in the house when he carried out the work on the bungalow and later wondered if this had something to do with its late detection of the fire.)

Black smoke was filling the house as Andrew stumbled out of bed. He called the fire service and then did everything he could to tame the blaze himself. When the emergency services arrived he had to be treated for smoke inhalation, but it's fair to say Hugo's actions to wake him up saved Andrew from further injury.

It turned out that an electrical fault was responsible for the fire and the firefighters made it clear what a vital role Hugo had played in saving Andrew and his house.

Andrew said: "The fire chief said that I had better buy the cat a big piece of fish because he saved my life. I'm just so thankful to that little fella."

JACK: THE TERRITORIAL TABBY

Jack the ginger tabby cat sprung to fame in 2006 when he saw off a black bear that had wandered into his owner Donna's back yard in West Milford, New Jersey, USA. Black bears are often spotted here, and residents treat the creatures with both respect and caution, aware of how to handle such a situation should it occur.

So while this bear sighting was not uncommon, what was unusual was Jack's reaction to it. Little Jack squared up to the bear, hissing and spitting to such a degree that the terrified animal darted toward the nearest tree and headed straight up it. There was no way Jack was going to let this big beast stomp into his territory and endanger his owner.

Bearing in mind (pun intended) that an adult black bear can weigh anything between 90 and 270 kilograms – and Jack the tabby clocked in at just 7 kilograms – helps you to build a picture of this scenario. Adopted from a cat rescue shelter a decade previously and declawed, Jack was not exactly a youthful feline, but he more than made up for it when it came to protecting his patch.

Tiny-but-mighty Jack so terrified the bear that it clung to the tree branches, hiding from its furry nemesis, for a good 15 minutes. The bear eventually crept back down the tree to make a break for it, only to be confronted by Jack once more and chased up a different tree. This time Jack was taking no chances and sat at the base of the trunk, glaring up at the bear among the branches. The poor bear no doubt rued the day it had decided to wander into this particular back yard and cowered up the tree for as long as Jack waited below.

Worried about her pet, Donna called to Jack and was able to coax him into the house. The frightened bear saw its chance and made its way back down the tree before bolting into the nearby woods and out of sight.

Donna's neighbour even managed to capture the incident via a series of photographs, showing fearless Jack at the base of the tree, looking up at the hulking great bear attempting to hide among the leaves.

Jack clearly felt a duty of care to his family who had loved and nurtured him – he wanted to protect them from the unwanted garden visitor.

Donna was interviewed by the local paper about territorial Jack's escapades with the bear and simply said: "He doesn't want anybody in his yard." Bears included.

JASPER AND WILLOW: COMFORT IN DIFFICULT TIMES

Jasper and Willow were named joint National Cats of the Year in 2022 by the National Cat Awards in the UK for their services to the patients of a hospice in Haywards Heath, West Sussex.

The brother-and-sister pair of rescue cats were recognized for the daily joy they bring to residents of the St Peter & St James Hospice in southeastern England.

Staff adopted the cats to bring some comfort and companionship to patients receiving end-of-life care. Not only were the mogs up to the job, but they also provided vital support for those visiting family and friends at the hospice – and indeed staff during stressful days for them.

Front-of-house manager Jackie Manville said: "Since they've been with us, they've brought comfort to so many people, whether it's patients, family and friends, or staff. Jasper and Willow really go to show how special rescue cats are, and we're so proud of them both."

A cat on a lap can provide a great deal of comfort and pleasure to those experiencing end-of-life care. Jackie explains: "Jasper in particular seems to intuitively know when patients are having a difficult day or if they are in need of company. He'll hop onto the bed and just sit quietly, purring away. It's enough to raise a smile and helps people relax when they're feeling tense and worried. For the staff too, having Jasper and Willow around is wonderful. On a hard day, just walking around the corner and seeing them is enough to give you a lift."

The pair also took home the Outstanding Rescue Cat accolade; awards judge and *Dragons' Den* star Deborah Meaden explained why: "It's amazing to see how two rescue cats are now so happy and comfortable in their role of comforting others who are going through very difficult times. If ever cats can show empathy, these two do."

KIDDO: THE AIRSHIP CAT

Back in 1910 Kiddo was a former stray who, along with his brother, lived in and around an airship hangar in New Jersey, USA. The grey tabby had been adopted by one of the crew members of Walter Wellman's airship *America*, which was about to embark on a potentially record-breaking voyage.

Wellman was an American journalist, explorer and aeronaut, and had persuaded three newspapers across the world – Britain's *Daily Telegraph*, *The New York Times* and *The Chicago Record-Herald* – to finance a new venture of his. He hoped to become the first person to cross the Atlantic Ocean by air.

Just as the airship was about to take off, a last-minute decision was made to take Kiddo on board and he was lifted into the lifeboat underneath the airship.

As the airship took off, it flew straight into dense fog. Kiddo was not a fan and howled and meowed while running about "like a squirrel in a cage". Kiddo got on the nerves of first engineer Melvin Vaniman and in a historic moment (*America* was the first aircraft to have radio equipment on board) the first in-flight radio message to be delivered to land was: "Roy, come and get this goddamn cat!"

While *America*'s navigator thought he should stay as a good luck charm, the rest of the crew voted to return Kiddo to shore. The cat was placed in a canvas bag and lowered below the airship where a motorboat tried to retrieve him. However, the mission was aborted due to bad weather and Kiddo was hauled back up into the airship's lifeboat once more.

Kiddo's behaviour improved and the crew soon deemed him "more useful than any barometer". Murray said: "You must never cross the Atlantic in an airship without a cat … This cat has always indicated trouble well ahead."

Kiddo became agitated in rough weather and howled so loudly that Murray proclaimed he had "never heard a cat make such a noise".

Sadly, the journey had to be abandoned when weather worsened and *America* experienced engine problems. The cat and crew climbed into the lifeboat attached to the underside of the airship and released it. The airship promptly "shot skyward" and was never seen again. The crew were rescued by British steamship RMS *Trent*, which hauled the lifeboat aboard. Kiddo was discovered to be fast asleep.

The Trent's captain, C. E. Down, sent a message to New York: "At 5 a.m. today sighted Wellman's airship *America* in distress … After three hours' manoeuvring and fresh winds blowing, got Wellman with his entire crew and cat. Were hauled safely on board. All are well."

Arriving in New York, *America*'s crew were met by a crowd of well-wishers. While they might not have completed their voyage, *America* had still broken records by remaining in the air for almost 72 hours and covering more than a thousand miles.

Kiddo was renamed Trent, in honour of the rescue steamship, and became something of a celebrity. He was displayed for a time in leading department store Gimbel's, where he napped and lounged on soft cushions in a gilded cage. Gimbel's made a fortune from picture postcards of Kiddo.

Kiddo eventually retired from the spotlight and lived out his last days with Wellman's daughter Edith.

Kiddo might have achieved several firsts, but he wasn't the first mog to be airborne. Some 130 years previously, in 1785, Vincenzo Lunardi demonstrated a hydrogen-filled balloon flight over London with a dog, cat and caged pigeon on board.

Nine years after Walter Wellman and Kiddo's failed attempt, in 1919, a tabby kitten named Wopsie (later renamed Jazz) stowed away with his owner William Ballantyne on a British airship, becoming the very first feline to make a trans-Atlantic crossing by air. While hiding in a cramped space, William became ill and was forced to confess to the crew he had stowed away. He was cared for and allowed to rest, going on to work as a cook to earn his keep aboard the airship. Wopsie, however, became the airship's mascot until it crashed two years later. All crew survived and Wopsie escaped with a bruised paw.

KOSHKA: THE FACE OF HOPE

Jesse Knott was a US Army sergeant posted in the Maiwand district of southern Afghanistan. In 2010, the country was a dangerous place, ravaged by years of violence. Jesse had previously served on the front line in Iraq, so was well used to the hostilities of war-torn environments. Even so, he was doing his best to stay strong in these stressful conditions.

Not long after Jesse arrived, he came across a little stray cat who was making regular visits to the US Army base. The cat was friendly, but a little nervous. Jesse noticed that it often turned up with paint on its fur or cuts on its back and he began to wonder if it was being mistreated. One day the mog appeared with a badly injured paw and Jesse decided enough was enough. He made it his personal mission to help his new furry friend out of the abusive situation he was in and keep him safe from harm. Jesse patched up the cat's paw and named him Koshka, Russian for "cat".

Koshka was assigned a safe corner of Jesse's office and the sergeant cherished his friendship with the animal, who in the midst of war provided a reminder of normality and his life back home. Jesse said: "You lose faith in a lot, but sometimes it's the smallest things that bring you back."

Six months later, a suicide bomb attack killed two of Jesse's friends and injured countless others. Jesse hit rock bottom, but Koshka provided a source of great comfort in his darkest hour. Jesse said: "I had tears in my eyes. He locked eyes with me, reached out with his paw and pressed it to my lips. Then he climbed down and into my lap, curled up and shared the moment with me. I'd lost all hope in myself; I'd lost faith. Then all of a sudden this cat came over and it was like, 'Hey, you're you.' He pulled me out of one of my darkest times, so I had to pull him out of one of his darkest places."

And with that, Jesse vowed to ensure the cat had a future in a safer place. Jesse was about to be redeployed so had to act fast. In stepped the Afghan Stray Animal League shelter in Kabul, which agreed to take in Koshka and ensure his safe passage to America, where he could make a new home with Jesse. Kabul, however, was halfway across the country – a severely unstable country across which travel was far from safe.

A local translator came to their rescue – with plans to travel to see family in Kabul, he agreed to take Koshka with him. This was a perilous journey for both of them – translating was not viewed favourably by the Taliban and had the brave volunteer been stopped at a checkpoint he would have likely been killed.

Jesse waited nervously for several days to hear news of Koshka's arrival in Kabul and was overjoyed to hear both he and the translator were safe. Koshka was taken in by the shelter, vaccinated and issued with papers.

Jesse's friends and family rallied around and raised the $3,000 needed to get Koshka to the United States. Several flights later and Koshka arrived in his new home of Portland,

Oregon. The pair were awarded the Oregon Humane Society's Diamond Collar Hero Award, recognizing pets and people for "remarkable achievements".

KUNKUSH: AN EPIC JOURNEY

Kunkush was a three-year-old white Turkish Van cat, who made the treacherous journey with his human family – a mother and her five children – from Iraq to Lesbos, Greece. They travelled in a rubber dinghy to flee the violence in their homeland and find a better, safer life.

The beloved pet was carried by his family in a basket, but upon arrival Kunkush grew scared and ran off to hide on the beach.

The family looked high and low for their precious cargo. They had gone to great lengths to bring him with them, but eventually had to give up their search and head to a refugee camp.

A few days later in a local fishing village, a dishevelled and rather sandy white cat appeared. Some local fishermen took it upon themselves to feed the little cat and named him Dias, modern Greek for "Zeus". While there was a rumour the cat had arrived on a boat with a refugee family, no one knew how to contact them to return him. The fishermen had taken a shine to this moggy who had travelled so far and took him to a local vet to be checked over.

News of the cat now known as Dias spread, as people heard the story of how he had travelled so far and in such perilous conditions only to be separated from his loved ones on arrival. Ashley Anderson, an American volunteer with a refugee charity, was determined to return Dias to his family and along with some friends devised a strong social media campaign. Dias' plight had its own Facebook page as Ashley and her friends tried desperately to reach anyone who might know the whereabouts of the cat's family.

While the search was on, Dias needed somewhere to live, so a foster family was found for him in Berlin. The money for his flight was raised through crowdfunding and the donations of a host of generous animal lovers, then Dias was assigned an EU passport and made the journey to his new home in Germany.

Two months later, word came from Norway when someone reached out via Facebook; they were certain that this cat was in fact Kunkush, whom they had heard many stories of from their new Iraqi neighbours, who had moved in recently. The family had spoken of their heartbreak at having travelled so far with their beloved pet only to lose him when they reached land. An exchange of photographs between Ashley and the family only confirmed the likeness.

Kunkush was put on a video call with his family and, confused, kept looking behind the computer screen for them. A further round of crowdfunding later and the little lost cat was on a plane to Norway for the last leg of his journey. It was an emotional reunion that was captured by a Norwegian television camera crew. Kunkush's owners were overjoyed to see him again, and the mother of the family wept and cried out: "Kunkush, my life!"

LADY: ALL EARS

In January 2020, a stray was picked up by the Dane County Humane Society in Wisconsin, USA. Due to an infection, she had to have her ear flaps removed.

Christened Lady in a Fur Coat, or Lady for short, the soft grey cat was friendly and cuddly, but she never seemed to be first in line for adoption when prospective owners came to visit the shelter.

Ash Collins, who worked at the Humane Society, thought she might have the answer. Skilled with a crochet needle and a ball of yarn, Ash crocheted a set of purple-and-white ears with a strap that tied perfectly under Lady's chin.

Mere hours after the shelter shared photos on social media of Lady with her new set of ears she was snapped up for adoption. Other social media users posted photos of their own cats with missing ear flaps due to similar medical issues. Perhaps they were after a set of crocheted ears for their feline friends too? There was a flood of support for these cats and multiple cries of how beautiful they all were.

Ash said: "Staff and volunteers at Dane County Humane Society consistently go above and beyond for the animals in our care. I was more than happy to use my crochet skills to help Lady stand out and get the second chance she deserved, and I'm so honoured to be a small part of her happy ending."

LARRY: THE DOWNING STREET CAT

Possibly the most famous cat in the UK is Larry, the tabby-and-white cat who lives at 10 Downing Street in London, formal residence of the British Prime Minister. Officially "Chief Mouser to the Cabinet Office", Larry was appointed in 2011 and has been in charge of pest control at the famous address ever since.

Having been a stray on the streets of London, Larry was a resident of Battersea Dogs and Cats Home when the shelter was tasked with providing a cat up to the ultimate mousing challenge. Larry's strong predatory instinct had been observed by his carers, so it was a no-brainer when it came to selecting a mog to serve the country.

Larry was immediately popular with both staff and the public, and is often photographed outside Number 10 or spotted perched on the doorstep behind news presenters reporting from Downing Street.

According to the Downing Street website, "Larry spends his days greeting guests to the house, inspecting security defences and testing antique furniture for napping quality."

Poor Larry faced some backlash about the latter activity and when, after two months in residence, he had not yet made a kill, he was accused of being lazy and spending too much time snoozing and hanging around with local cat Masie. He soon silenced his critics with his first catch and, a year later in 2012, made his first public kill in front of the press outside Number 10. Larry ceremoniously abandoned the dead mouse on the famous doorstep and has held on to public respect ever since.

David Cameron, who was prime minister of the UK when Larry came to reside at Downing Street, once told press that Larry was skittish and nervous around men – possibly alluding to poor treatment by a male owner during his earlier years. However, when US President Barack Obama visited the UK in 2016, Larry made an exception and the two became firm friends. Cameron said: "Obama gave him a stroke and he was OK with Obama."

When Cameron left office in 2016 and departed the famous address, Larry stayed on to keep up his important mousing work. He has since served four prime ministers: Theresa May, Boris Johnson, Liz Truss and Rishi Sunak, and will no doubt do his duty for future premiers.

The famous cat recently celebrated 12 years of mousing in Downing Street, his length of service eclipsing those of former prime ministers Benjamin Disraeli, Winston Churchill, Margaret Thatcher and Tony Blair, not to mention the aforesaid Conservative PMs under whom he served.

Larry has accounts across several social media platforms. With an almighty 838,000 followers on Twitter and healthy fan bases on Instagram and Facebook, Larry has even tried to attract Gen Z with a TikTok account that has racked up 2.2 million views.

Other chief mousers in residence at 10 Downing Street over the years have included Peter (and possibly Peter II and III), who served Prime Ministers Ramsay MacDonald,

Stanley Baldwin, Neville Chamberlain, Winston Churchill and Clement Atlee from 1929–46; Peta, who pest-controlled for Alec Douglas-Home, Edward Heath and Harold Wilson from 1964–76; Wilberforce, who was in place under Heath, Wilson (during his third term), Jim Callaghan and Margaret Thatcher from 1973–88; Humphrey, who served Thatcher, John Major and Tony Blair from 1989–97; and Sybil, who was chief mouser for Gordon Brown from 2007–09.

The White House, the serving US president's residence, has also had several feline inhabitants who have captured the hearts of those working and residing in the famous building. President Abraham Lincoln brought his cats Dixie and Tabby to live at the White House, and toward the end of the Civil War he also adopted three orphaned kittens. Theodore Roosevelt's cats Slippers and Tom Quartz came to live with him while he served; Calvin Coolidge brought his cats Blackie, Smokie, Tiger and Timmy with him; and Bill Clinton made his mogs Buddy and Socks join him in his presidential abode. President Joe Biden met grey tabby Willow when she wandered on stage during one of his campaign speeches. It wasn't long before he adopted her and named her after his hometown – Willow Grove, Pennsylvania.

Did you know?

In addition to the upper and lower eyelids, cats have a third eyelid in the corner of each eye toward the centre of the face. This eyelid is called the nictitating membrane and is usually hidden from view unless the cat is very relaxed or particularly sleepy. The third eyelid usually retracts as soon as the cat is awake and alert, but if it does not this could be a sign of a medical issue.

LUCKY: THE CALMING CAT

Lucky was a dark-grey-and-white shorthair rescue cat who brought joy into her new owners' lives, spreading harmony through their home and protecting them as best she could.

Giselle lived with her daughter Ahnya in Maryland, USA. Giselle noticed early on that Ahnya behaved differently to other kids – her speech was very advanced even when she was only a year old and she loved order, stacking boxes and books wherever she went, and even rearranging the shelves in the supermarket. While all kids experience meltdowns, to Giselle Ahnya's seemed to be next-level, would cause her untold distress and sometimes last for hours at a time.

When Ahnya was five, Giselle went to pick her up after a swimming lesson and was greeted by a stressed and very wet instructor. Asserting that she could already swim, Ahnya had apparently jumped into the deep end on her own several times. She didn't understand why she was doing anything wrong, but her mum cancelled the swimming lessons for obvious reasons.

Along with these behaviours, Ahnya displayed high anxiety and, while she excelled in reading and writing, she had no interest in socializing with other kids. Giselle took Ahnya to the doctor and she was diagnosed with autism spectrum disorder (ASD). Ahnya was enrolled in a school alongside other children with ASD, where she thrived.

When she was 11 years old, Ahnya was diagnosed with Tourette's syndrome.

Ahnya had begged Giselle for a pet cat for years. So when Ahnya was 12, Giselle decided it was the right time to give it a try. A big, white, fluffy cat named Snowball at their local shelter caught their attention and they booked a visit immediately. When they arrived, however, it was a different, four-year-old, grey-and-white shorthair cat named Lucky who stole their hearts. It was a tough decision, but the pair agreed they wanted to adopt Lucky.

When they got Lucky home, Giselle realized she had never seen her daughter so happy or excited. The cat settled in at their home quickly and had a dramatic impact almost immediately. Giselle was amazed to see the change in Ahnya's behaviour that came from having Lucky around. Her anxiety levels were much improved just by being in the company of the beautiful cat.

Giselle said: "I noticed that when Ahnya's anxiety was high and she was screaming or crying, Lucky would appear from nowhere. I would say, 'Be careful, don't scare Lucky', and almost immediately Ahnya would calm right down and snuggle with the cat."

Giselle recalled the way Lucky was able to diffuse a particularly tricky situation: "I remember we had only had Lucky two weeks when Ahnya had a screaming fit about not being able to find the charger to her tablet. I knew it was a bad one because she was hitting her head with her hand and screaming so loud. It was very distressing to see and none of our usual breathing techniques were working. Lucky came and sat on a side table, then jumped on Ahnya on the couch. Ahnya was screaming the place down and Lucky stood on her back legs and pawed her until she stopped and smiled. Then Lucky put her paw on Ahnya's thigh and that was it, all over. I couldn't believe my eyes!"

The effect Lucky has on Ahnya is remarkable and Giselle is ever grateful they brought the little grey-and-white cat home with them that day. She said: "I was amazed at how Lucky was instantly able to bring Ahnya back to me so quickly. It was as if any time Ahnya was in distress, Lucky picked up on her emotions and was there to love and support her during every single screaming fit. A lot of the time Lucky wasn't an overly affectionate cat, preferring to do her own thing, but when Ahnya needed her she was always there. It was like watching a miracle unfolding in front of my eyes."

LUIGI: THE LONG JOURNEY HOME

Luigi was a Scottish Fold kitten, bought when he was seven weeks old as a gift by Sebastian Smetham for his partner Finn. The couple lived in Barcelona, Spain, with their six-year-old pug dog Bandito, so Luigi was the perfect addition to their little family. Much to the couple's delight, Bandito and Luigi got on famously and immediately became good friends.

Sebastian and Finn felt a shift in their family when Luigi came to join them, as if he was guiding them in a certain direction. They credit Luigi with the decisions they made that led them to re-evaluate their lives.

Sebastian said: "When Luigi arrived, he seemed to take charge. It was him and Bandito who led us on this journey to find a better life for them and us. Which we did."

The couple decided to leave their life in Barcelona behind and, taking their beloved animals with them and armed with a tent and a dog trolley, set off for northern Spain to walk the Camino de Santiago.

The Camino de Santiago – translated as "the Way of St James" – is a network of pilgrims' routes across northern Spain more than 460 miles long, which ultimately leads to the shrine of St James in the Cathedral of Santiago de Compostela in Galicia.

Sebastian, Finn, Bandito and Luigi took three months to make their way from one end of the route to the other, and all four of them took to the lifestyle straight away. This was particularly surprising for Luigi as cats are notoriously territorial, preferring their home turf and being sensitive to changes in their surroundings. Luigi, however, seemed suited to life on the road and was happy to travel in the trolley or on top of one of his owners' backpacks.

The four travellers all slept in a tent together and Luigi particularly began to display real affection for nature, much preferring leaf and bug chasing to any of the cat toys his owners had bought for him.

The young cat did a lot of growing up on the road, learning to climb trees and hunt, and even being neutered while the family were travelling. They stopped at a campsite for several days following this procedure to allow Luigi some recovery time.

The epic journey across Spain gave Sebastian and Finn much time to consider what they wanted from their future and the space to re-evaluate. They decided to make the move from Barcelona to Marbella and set up home with their pets, who were happy to all have each other.

Sebastian said: "It was Luigi and Bandito's relationship that made it possible. They are inseparable and one without the other would never have worked. They look after each other and also fight like brothers – or like cats and dogs!"

MAJOR TOM:
THE CAPTAIN'S CAT

Major Tom was a black-and-white cat that lived aboard his owner's yacht *Osprey*. Grant McDonald had been living on his vessel with his feline pal for six years, off the coast of Australia.

Every night before going to bed, Grant would carry out a series of checks around the boat to ensure all was well before he settled down for a good night's sleep on the water. In the early hours of one morning in September 2015, Grant was woken up by Major Tom repeatedly headbutting him. Grant wasn't sure why his cat was behaving in this way, but whatever was bothering him seemed urgent.

Grant decided to run through his checklist again for good measure and discovered the bow of the boat was much lower than usual. Panic rose as Grant realized the vessel was letting in water fast. Grant realized it was too dark and too dangerous to attempt to investigate the leak himself and had to make the snap decision to raise the alarm and get himself and Major Tom onto a life raft as quickly as possible.

Grant and his cat huddled together for warmth on the life raft while they waited for help. Eight long hours passed before they were rescued by Chinese bulk carrier *Shi Dai 8*, which had made a diversion to come to Grant and Major Tom's aid.

Major Tom was lifted to safety and Grant followed his feline friend. After a spell in hospital where he was treated for shock, Grant was reunited with his cat.

The pair lost everything that was onboard *Osprey* that day, as well as their home, but most importantly they still had each other.

MASHA: THE BABY WHISPERER

One freezing night in the Kaluga region of Russia, local stray Masha the long-haired tabby did something remarkable as well as sounding the alarm when someone vulnerable needed help.

In this part of Russia residents are always prepared when winter rolls around and brings with it temperatures of well below zero. The conditions can be lethal if you fail to take precautions and don't have the right clothing.

Local resident Nadezhda Makhovikova was in her apartment when she heard a noise in the stairwell. She discovered it to be a cat, meowing loudly and urgently from a cardboard box.

She couldn't believe her eyes when she peered over the rim of the box and saw Masha curled around a baby, who was sleeping in the box. Masha had heard the baby crying and had sought to comfort him by climbing into the box, warming him against her fur and licking his face to soothe him.

Nadezhda called the emergency services at once, aware the baby might need medical attention urgently.

Masha clearly felt a strong urge to protect the baby and showed signs of distress when the little human was taken away in an ambulance.

Paramedic Vera Ivanina, who arrived on the scene, said Masha ran after her as she carried the baby to the waiting ambulance: "She was so worried about where we were taking him. She ran right behind us, meowing."

In hospital, the baby was found to be in great health, and the authorities started the search for his parents. Masha was credited with playing a large part in saving the little boy's life and was showered with treats by the building's residents.

MICKEY:
UNWAVERING SUPPORT

The love of Christine Leinonen's life was her son Christopher. When he was growing up it was just the two of them and they were close, so when Christopher came out as gay to Christine, she couldn't have been more proud of her son for sharing this with her.

Christopher was an activist in high school, setting up the first Gay–Straight Alliance group, and won the first Anne Frank Humanitarian Award. When he went to study at the University of Central Florida, Christine moved to be closer to her son.

Christopher later became a mental health counsellor in the Orlando Hospital Emergency Room. In 2015 he fell in love with Juan and Christine was a big fan, finding him to be a "kind and loving young man who adored Christopher". The pair lived happily in Orlando together and Christine resided just an hour away.

On 12 June 2016, Christopher and Juan went out to the Pulse nightclub in Orlando and never came home. A local security guard, later deemed to be a terrorist, opened fire on the crowd of revellers, leaving 49 people dead and more than 50 wounded in what has been referred to as the worst mass-shooting in recent US history. Christopher died in the club that night and Juan passed away in hospital from his injuries.

Christine was grief stricken and shut herself off from the rest of the world. She found it difficult to answer the phone, which kept ringing as people reached out to offer support. In this dark time, she found loving comfort in the shape of her black-and-white cat Mickey.

Mickey had entered Christine's life in 2012, when her mother Minnie had passed away. She decided that adopting a cat would help with the grief; however, when Christine visited the Polk County animal shelter she immediately became besotted with twin black-and-white kittens, a boy and a girl. She had originally only intended to go home with one cat that day, but after playing with the sweet pair she didn't see how she could leave with one and not the other. To honour her mother, Christine named the female kitten Minnie and the male Mickey, naturally.

A while later, Christine had taken in another stray, Cracker. While Mickey was indifferent to the new arrival, Minnie couldn't stand a new feline on her patch and made it known whenever she could. Christine eventually had to make a tough call and rehome Minnie with a friend, where she was far happier being the only cat of the house.

Christine missed Minnie's presence – she had always been the affectionate one of the feline siblings, with Mickey more standoffish and independent – not a cuddly cat in the slightest.

So in 2016, when Christine was again wracked with grief, something in Mickey changed. He became loyal and loving when he saw Christine needed him to be.

Mickey began to approach Christine when she wept, sitting on her lap and forcing his head up to her hand to make her pet him when she was in a state of grief. His loving actions gave Christine something else to focus on when the pain surged.

Christine said: "The very feel of him on my knee and the petting action helped me to calm down, to gather my breath and to look at this beautiful animal on my lap. Not only did he calm me down, but Mickey also reminded me that I had to get back the will to live again."

By this point she had taken on another stray – Teenie – and Mickey helped her see that she needed to stay strong to look after her furry family. She said: "Here he was showing me the unconditional love that I had always felt toward Christopher and I needed it so much."

Christine eventually channelled her grief into activism and became an outspoken voice on gun control, believing that had there been tighter laws, the type of firearm that killed her son might not have been accessible to the perpetrator.

She remains close to her cat: "Mickey saved my life," she said. "I still have hard times but they are getting fewer, yet when I do he's always with me, like he instinctively knows I'm going to need him."

MIKE: THE MUSEUM CAT

The British Museum in London, UK, has a long history of cat residents – its most famous was housed in 1909.

Keeper of Egyptian Antiquities, Sir Ernest Wallis Budge, was leaving his residence one morning when monochrome Black Jack, a frequent feline visitor to the museum, dropped a kitten at his feet. Ernest was baffled when Black Jack strolled away, leaving the tiny fluffball on the doorstep. Ernest named the kitten Mike and put him to work as one of the British Museum cats, chasing away pests and keeping order about the place. The cats were well looked after and fed cooked meat every day.

Mike became a much-loved feline face around the museum. Black Jack taught him how to apprehend pigeons by slowly driving them into a corner. Mike would apparently "point" at pigeons with his nose, much like a dog, while Black Jack rounded them up. Once the birds were cornered, each cat would grab one and take it to the housekeeper who would pay the cats in treats. The cats never harmed the pigeons, which were always safely released back onto the London streets.

Ernest and Mike had a special relationship, and Mike got on well with the gate staff too, who permitted him to sleep on a draught-free shelf in the Lodge. Even during World War One's acute shortages, the refreshment room staff would often give Mike milk and scraps.

He retired in 1924, after 15 years of service to the museum, but continued to live in the grounds. Ernest quit museum duties around the same time, but continued to visit his beloved cat companion and even contributed sixpence a week toward his upkeep. You could say that fearless Mike only semi-retired as he continued to chase stray dogs from the museum courtyard by puffing himself up to twice his usual size and throwing himself in their direction. Dogs were terrified of him and fled immediately.

Especially in his later years, Mike was not a fan of strangers and dodged any unwanted strokes by leaping up to the pediment above the lodge door. He did this so often the surface was apparently worn smooth by his solace seeking.

Late in life, Mike's teeth became severely decayed and he found it harder to eat. Such was the love for this cat around the museum that the gatekeepers would cook him tender meat and fish that he could manage. Apparently Mike "preferred sole to whiting, and whiting to haddock, and sardines to herring; while for cod he had no use whatsoever".

When he could no longer eat it was decided that the kindest thing to do would be to put him to sleep. He died in January 1929, at the ripe old age of 20. Assistant keeper in the British Museum's department of printed books F. C. W. Hiley wrote a poem in tribute to dear Mike entitled "To the Memory of 'Mike', the Museum Cat", an excerpt of which is on the next page.

So out of all the human crew
He cared for none – save only two:
For these he purred, for these he played,
And let himself be stroked, and laid
Aside his anti-human grudge –
His owner – and Sir Ernest Budge!
A master of Egyptian lore,
No doubt Sir Ernest had a store
Of charms and spells deciphered
From feline mummies long since dead,
And found a way by magic art
To win that savage feline heart.
Each morn Sir Ernest, without qualms,
Would take up Michael in his arms;
And still remained his staunchest friend,
And comforted his latter end.

MILO: FIRM FAMILY SUPPORT

Milo became part of the Smith family in 2020 and has provided unwavering support for all its members ever since.

Sue Smith, from Doncaster, UK, wouldn't be without the black-and-white moggy, after he stuck by her through her breast cancer diagnosis and treatment. The two-year-old family pet was a reassuring and comforting presence throughout a difficult time, especially as the pandemic was in full force, and Sue was unable to seek solace in the company of extended family and friends.

She said: "The treatment was hard enough and having it during lockdown made it even harder. But having Milo in my life was such a huge help. He was a wonderful distraction – always up to something entertaining! He made each day that little bit easier and during such a long and lonely year, he was a wonderful companion."

Sue isn't the only member of the family to have experienced Milo's impeccable bedside manner. He gets on particularly well with the family's dog, pug-chihuahua Max – the pair are inseparable and Milo likes to join in and learn tricks when Max is learning. Sue said: "When we've taught Max tricks like high-fives and to give a paw, Milo will join in!"

When Max had surgery on his knee and was confined to a cage he was experiencing cabin fever, but Milo was there for his canine friend. "Milo didn't leave his side," said Sue.

Milo is also a source of unending love and support for Sue's son who has ASD (autism spectrum disorder). "Milo is my son's best friend, and they're never far apart," said Sue. "The first thing he does when he comes home from school is find Milo. If he is feeling overwhelmed or stressed, he'll spend some time with Milo and it will help him feel more grounded. Milo is patient and loving, and my son takes great care of him, making sure he has everything he needs."

Milo's loyalty and support for the Smith family was recognized when he was shortlisted for the National Cat Awards, which looks to "celebrate real-life stories of heroism, loyalty and companionship in the feline world".

MINKA AND FRANCIS: FIRM FRIENDS

On a farm near Edmonton, Canada, lived a semi-feral cat, welcomed by the owners for her ability to keep the local rodent population under control. The one-year-old feline had a litter of kittens and the big farm barn had become home to the young family.

In the summer of 2021, the barn caught fire with the young kittens inside. The mother cat ran into the barn in a desperate attempt to save her babies, only to run out again without them. Bravely she ran into the blaze again and again, eventually emerging with just one of the kittens – a tiny black fluffball with white paws, who was unharmed. Tragically, she was unable to save the other kittens from the fiery barn.

The mother cat was badly injured in the rescue attempt, sustaining severe burns to her body, including her paw pads and ears. She had also inhaled a lot of smoke as she ran into the barn time and time again, and needed urgent medical treatment that the owners of the farm were unable to afford.

In stepped a local animal rescue shelter named Furget Me Not. The shelter was almost full, but owner Christine Koltun couldn't stand by when these two cats were so in need. She said: "When there's emergency situations like that, no matter how full we are I always do my best and my fosters are so wonderful. We kind of figure it out as we go. We just can't let cats like that suffer."

The staff named the mother Minka and kitten Francis. *Minka* translates from Polish as "strong-willed warrior" and, as Christine said, "It seemed very fitting for this mama!"

Minka was treated for her raw, open wounds and given something for the pain. Following a thorough assessment, she was sedated, given antibiotics and had her lungs X-rayed to check the damage from the smoke inhalation. While she was left physically scarred by the injuries she sustained in the fire, remarkably there was no sign that Minka would have any long-term health issues.

Minka and Francis were neutered, microchipped and vaccinated, and the pair were adopted together by a loving family. While unusual for mother cats and their kittens to be adopted together, this home set-up was quite fitting for Minka and Francis.

Christine said: "Usually the mother wants nothing to do with her kittens once they're weaned, but Minka was only about eight months herself when she had kittens, so they really grew up together and became great friends!"

MINTY: FAMILY SUPPORT

When Siobhan Cobb rescued three-legged white cat Minty, she couldn't have known the profound effect the cat would have on her family. After being injured in a road accident, Minty was given a second chance at life at her forever home with the Cobbs in Hollywell, Wales.

Siobhan's six-year-old son Connor has severe learning difficulties, as well as ataxic cerebral palsy, which affects his physical, mental and emotional development. The ways Minty has helped Connor to cope with life have been remarkable. The caring cat helps to keep him settled at mealtimes and is always on hand to nuzzle him and help to calm him down when he has an emotional meltdown. Minty is a pacifying influence over Connor at bedtime, always by his side and ready to help him get through this tricky stage of the day.

Minty even helped Connor learn how to climb the stairs, which, due to developmental issues, he was finding particularly difficult and needed extra help with. Siobhan says the pair share a "special bond". "Minty demonstrates how clever, affectionate and dependable cats can be. We can always rely on him to make everything better, and he is the best friend that Connor needs and deserves," she adds.

He might be one leg down, but that doesn't stop Minty from making the most of life and offering untold emotional support to Connor and the family. Siobhan says: "Having only three legs never stops Minty enjoying life, and I think that rubs off on Connor. Together, they are unstoppable, whatever comes their way. Minty's a really inspirational cat and we love him to bits."

Minty's dedication to the Cobb family was recognized at the National Cat Awards 2021 when he was awarded Cat of the Year – the highest honour that can be bestowed on a cat in the UK.

Comedian and category judge Russell Kane said: "I truly believe cats aren't used enough in teaching companionship and therapeutic ways, and for me, Minty's story drives forward the argument that cats are wonderful creatures, not just for them being furry and being stroked, but for the emotional benefits, the teaching benefits and the assistance they can bring to people's lives."

Awards organizer Kate Bunting said: "Minty is an incredible cat and a very deserving winner of the National Cat of the Year. He goes to show the life-changing and incredible bond which can be shared between children and cats. Minty has never let his own challenges stand in his way, and his zest for life is clear to see. Like many cats, Minty loves to be in the thick of family life, and we're so pleased that Connor has such a great friend by his side."

MITTENS: CAT IN THE CITY

Mittens is a beige-and-white Turkish Angora cat who for a while was a huge celebrity in the city of Wellington, New Zealand. Mittens would wander around the Te Aro area of the city and central business district, making scores of friends and fans along the way.

This intrepid feline was spotted anywhere and everywhere – from tattoo parlours to estate agents, a Latino salsa bar to the community law school, not to mention the university and various offices and churches.

Mittens was so well-loved and admired that a social media group was set up in his honour, racking up more than 65,000 followers. Fans would post photos of Mittens in unusual places around the city, while others would report sightings and some would even go hunting for the famous cat in the hope of snapping a selfie.

Despite his wandering, Mittens was a well-looked-after cat with an owner who loved him. Silvio Bruinsma said Mittens had similarly adventurous habits when they lived in Auckland but the compact nature of Wellington city centre made him easier to track and spot. Silvio has another Turkish Angora cat, Mittens' brother Latte. Latte, however, prefers to stick close to home, rarely venturing further than 65 feet from his front door – whereas Mittens has been known to roam as far as 1.25 miles.

Silvio said: "He has made Wellington his playground. I suppose my philosophy is, he doesn't like being locked up and I don't want to give him a life that is miserable."

New Zealand animal charity SPCA (Society for the Prevention of Cruelty to Animals) had to call on the Wellington public to ask them to stop bringing Mittens into their shelter worried for his well-being and concerned he was a stray.

One SPCA member said: "Please don't pick him up and bring him into SPCA. He has come in too many times with well-meaning people. All this means is that his owner has to come and collect him from us! We have had him in with us recently and he is perfectly healthy."

Mittens is so well monitored by the Wellington public that when he fell asleep in the corner of a shop, which locked its doors come closing time, the social media community rallied to track him down to his last known location and work out where he was. The owners of the store were alerted and were able to come back to the shop to let Mittens out.

Mittens is so well loved that he was awarded the keys to the city by Wellington Mayor Andy Foster and awarded with a certificate. The Wellington Museum also hosted a mini exhibition dedicated to Mittens, entitled *Mittens – Floofy and Famous*, featuring a host of photographs of Mittens out and about in the city adorning the walls and raising money for the SPCA Wellington Centre in the process.

Wellington residents mourned the departure of Mittens when Silvio decided to take his pets and return to Auckland. Relocated, but not forgotten.

MJ: BICYCLE MADE FOR TWO

Tabby cat MJ – short for Mary Jane – was a much-loved presence on the streets of Philadelphia, Pennsylvania, USA, perched atop her owner Rudi's shoulder as he delivered parcels throughout the city.

Along with her four siblings, MJ was born in a closet drawer in Rudi's house to her mother, who was just stopping by. The other kittens and their mother were found loving forever homes and MJ stayed put to become Rudi's first pet cat.

Rudi quickly discovered that MJ's favourite resting spot was on his shoulders. This gave him a brainwave – perhaps the cat could be his work companion. Rudi worked as a courier, delivering packages up and down the city streets of Philadelphia – a solitary job where a furry friend to keep him company on his shifts could be just what he needed.

Rudi had previously owned pet sugar gliders and trained these little creatures to sit on his shoulder on the move, so it felt like the natural thing to do. On day one, Rudi took MJ around the block on his shoulder. On day two she perched for two blocks. Before they knew it, MJ was accompanying Rudi for whole days as he zipped around the city covering 25 miles in a single shift.

Rudi said: "MJ enjoys the wind rushing through her fur and she moves around from shoulder to shoulder. She is so comfortable on my shoulder she never uses her claws. My shoulder and back are scratch-free."

Pedestrians on the city streets would often stop and stare at the furry passenger's unusual mode of transport, often amazed and regularly asking to take photos.

MJ really was right at home on the road, sat firmly on Rudi's shoulder, unbothered by the traffic. She was scared of noisy sirens, however, and wasn't the biggest fan of loud buses or growling motorbikes, so Rudi would do his best to zip away from those as quickly as he could.

MUSCHI: FRIEND OF THE BEARS

Some say black cats are a sign of good luck and this one was certainly a bringer of good fortune and unlikely friendship between species.

One day in 2000, at Berlin Zoo in Germany, a tiny black cat was spotted in the enclosure of Maeuschen, a black bear. Staff were understandably concerned – Maeuschen was known to be fairly gentle and at 35 years old was not the fastest animal, but she was still a black bear and there was every chance her instinct to attack might kick in.

But to the staff's delight and surprise, it did not. The pair warmed to one another and quickly became firm friends, spending their days side by side and sharing snacks. No one knew where the little cat had come from, so they decided to keep her and named her Muschi, which means "pussycat" in German.

Zoo staff member Heiner Kloes said: "Muschi appeared from nowhere and we decided to leave them together because they got on so well. They sunbathed together and shared meals of raw meat, dead mice, fruit and bread."

Due to Maeuschen's age, the pair led a fairly unenergetic existence, spending their days lazing together and snoozing in patches of sunshine.

The pair became popular with the public and attracted many visitors and donations, helping to elevate the zoo and pay for much-needed supplies.

In 2007, the big bear was moved to a temporary cage so her home enclosure could be refurbished. Muschi was so distraught at being separated from her much larger companion that she stood meowing outside the cage until staff relented and allowed her in to join Maeuschen. Kloes said: "They greeted each other, had a cuddle and were happy."

After an extraordinarily heart-warming friendship spanning a decade, sadly Maeuschen died in 2010 following years of health issues, coupled with arthritis. Muschi lived out the rest of her days at Berlin Zoo, cared for by the staff who never forgot the affection they had witnessed between these two remarkable creatures.

Did you know?

Cats have scent glands all over their bodies – around the mouth, chin, forehead, cheeks, lower back, tail and even on their paws. Anyone with a cat at home will find their abode has been marked from top to bottom as their feline companion's territory – and when they rub themselves up against their owners they are marking them too.

NALA: THE TRAVELLING CAT

Dean Nicholson left his home in Dunbar, Scotland, in September 2018 with a plan to cycle around the world. He had just turned 30 and was looking to experience new challenges and perhaps gain a fresh perspective along the way. He set up the Instagram account @1bike1world to document his epic journey and allow others to follow his progress.

Three months and nine countries later, Dean was travelling alone in the mountains of southern Bosnia, when he heard a noise behind him. A scrawny grey-and-white kitten was running along behind his bike, meowing with as much might as it could muster. According to Dean it had "sharply pointing ears, spindly legs and a thick tail" as well as big green eyes.

The tiny kitten fitted in the palm of Dean's hand and he was concerned for its safety out there on the road; it could have been potential roadkill or easy prey for a large bird unless he did something about it. So he scooped up the kitten and plopped her into the bag attached to the front of his bike.

Dean resumed cycling, but the kitten jumped out and climbed onto his shoulders where she fell asleep. He was quite smitten and named her Nala, after the character in *The Lion King*, a name that means "gift" in Swahili.

Dean registered Nala with a local vet and from then on she was his trusty travel companion. Dean said: "We were an unusual sight; a big, bearded tattooed bloke on a bike, with a kitten sitting on his shoulder like Long John Silver's parrot."

Nala stole the hearts of all the people they met along the way, however, and it wasn't long before the media wanted a piece of their story. All it took was for one website to run an article on the unlikely pair and Dean's Instagram following went from 3,000 to 150,000 overnight. Their adventures were picked up by more media outlets and then that number shot up to 800,000 across Instagram and YouTube.

The pair became celebrities and were often stopped in the street by strangers who wanted to chat about their extraordinary experiences and take photos. Dean realized that, with Nala's newfound fame, he could do something for others and set about raising money for local animal charities. A Nala calendar followed and the pair raised a whopping £90,000 for 30 charities.

Dean wrote a book about their travels to spread their remarkable story further and *Nala's World* was born. A children's version followed and it's fair to say the world was utterly charmed by their cycling escapades.

Dean said: "She not only changed my world. She changed the world around me."

OSCAR: THE UNSINKABLE CAT

Back in 1941, in the midst of World War Two, the German ship *Bismarck* set sail on its one and only mission. Nine days later, after engaging in a lengthy battle with British warships, *Bismarck* sank leaving only 118 survivors of its 2,200-strong crew.

The survivors were brought on board British vessel HMS *Cossack* and, amid the floating debris, a little black cat was spotted on a plank. The British established that the cat had resided on *Bismarck* before it sank and brought him aboard *Cossack*. He became the ship's mascot and the crew named him Oscar.

Several months passed with Oscar living happily aboard the *Cossack* as it carried out its convoy escort duties in the Mediterranean and north Atlantic. However, in October 1941, the ship was badly damaged by an explosion caused by a torpedo fired from a German submarine. The attack cost the lives of 159 of *Cossack*'s crew and its front section was destroyed. The ship began to sink. Along with the other surviving crew, Oscar was transferred to HMS *Legion*, which attempted to tow the damaged *Cossack* back to Gibraltar. It was not to be – *Cossack* sank three days later.

After being brought ashore, Oscar was nicknamed "Unsinkable Sam" for having survived yet another shipwreck. The cat with many lives continued his seafaring career aboard aircraft carrier HMS *Ark Royal* – which coincidentally was one of the ships which had a hand in sinking the *Bismarck*.

A mere two weeks later, *Ark Royal* was hit by a German torpedo and began to sink. Attempts to tow the ship once again failed and survivors were attended to. Oscar was spotted in the water hanging on to a floating plank; he was described as "angry, but quite unharmed".

Oscar boarded one final ship – HMS *Lightning* – with the rest of the survivors and was delivered to shore. He never set foot on a vessel again and spent the rest of the war on the base in Gibraltar, put to work catching mice around the naval offices.

When the war was over, Oscar retired to Belfast where he lived a quiet and happy life with a sailor, no doubt relieved to be on dry land and away from the potential of yet another shipwreck. He died in 1955.

If you ever visit the National Maritime Museum in Greenwich, London, UK, be sure to look out for the pastel portrait of our hero – *Oscar, cat from the German ship "Bismarck"*, by Georgina Shaw-Baker.

OZZIE: THE CAMPUS CAT

Ozzie, a 14-year-old black cat, is a popular character around campus at Newcastle University in the UK, garnering attention wherever he wanders. He is something of a social media sensation too, with more Instagram followers than the university's vice-chancellor has on Twitter.

Ozzie is said to be a calming influence around exam time, helping to ease anxieties when stress levels are running high, and students who miss their pets and might have relied on them for comfort and companionship get a lot out of Ozzie's presence. One student said: "Especially over exams, we saw her a few times in the library. It was a pretty stressful time so whenever she came in it was really nice."

At one point, Ozzie underwent surgery to have a malignant tumour removed and the support roles were somewhat reversed as the students stepped up to look out for their beloved feline. There was an outpouring of love on social media.

One student said: "We're all worried about Ozzie and trying to see her."

Another student said to Ozzie while handing her a treat: "We want to give you the best time while you have it."

University chaplain Mia Fox, Ozzie's owner, said: "She's been a bit poorly recently – she had mammary carcinoma, which is breast cancer. After her operation she got an awful lot of love back from the students. The kind comments and direct messages, and the love she's had back from the students has been quite amazing. And Ozzie's been answering them all."

PADDLES: THE FIRST CAT OF NEW ZEALAND

Paddles was the cat of former New Zealand Prime Minister Jacinda Ardern and her partner Clarke Gayford, who they adopted from a local branch of the SPCA (Society for the Protection of Cruelty to Animals). A ginger-and-white polydactyl cat (meaning she was born with more than the usual number of toes on her paws), Paddles had opposable thumbs – also unusual for a cat! – and gathered many fans as the "First Cat of New Zealand".

A Twitter account – @FirstCatofNZ – was mysteriously set up in her honour, with many joking she had been tech savvy enough to set it up herself with her opposable thumbs... Her Twitter profile read: "Paddles Ardern-Gayford. She/her. First Cat of New Zealand. Have thumbs, will tweet. Not affurliated with the Labour Pawty. Bullies will be scratched/blocked." The account soon filled up with tweets directed at other cats and dogs owned by world leaders, including Lennu, the Boston terrier dog belonging to Finnish president Sauli Niinistö, and Larry the cat who lives at 10 Downing Street in London, UK, the official residence of the UK prime minister.

Jacinda Ardern said of the social media account: "There is indeed an account in the name of my cat and I have no idea who has created it. I am quite happy for that person to continue logging on, on behalf of Paddles. Keeping in mind that Paddles has thumbs, I can't put it past her it's her own account as well."

Tragically, only a year after coming to live with Jacinda and Clarke, Paddles was hit by a car near their home and died before she could get the medical attention she needed. Paddles' death was announced on social media: "Very sad PR guy here. Thank you so much for loving Paddles, the whole world will mourn her. Not bad for a lil SPCA puss."

Ardern said on social media: "To anyone who has ever lost a pet, you'll know how sad we feel. Paddles was much loved and not just by us. Thanks for everyone's thoughts. And on behalf of Paddles, please be kind to the SPCA. They found her before we did and we will always be grateful for that."

Tributes poured in from across the globe, with Palmerston, the British Foreign Office cat tweeting: "My deepest condolences to @jacindaardern at this difficult time. @FirstCatofNZ did more in a short time than many do over a long career."

PALMERSTON: THE BRITISH FOREIGN OFFICE CAT

From 2016 until 2020, Palmerston was the resident chief mouser at the Foreign & Commonwealth Office in Whitehall, London, UK. Rescued from Battersea Dogs & Cats Home, Palmerston was considered an important addition to the staff in the government department, helping to rid the historic building of its ever-growing population of mice.

He was named after the popular nineteenth century Foreign Secretary and Prime Minister Viscount Palmerston, who was considered instrumental in the creation of the Divorce Court in 1857.

When feline Palmerston was appointed, Foreign Office bosses pointed out the black-and-white domestic shorthair would certainly not be a burden on the UK taxpayer. The department issued a pun-loaded statement that said: "Palmerston's domestic posting will have zero cost to the public purrse as a staff kitty will be used to pay for him and all aspects of his welfur."

Throughout his illustrious career as Foreign Office mouser, Palmerston has been caught sneaking into 10 Downing Street, official residence of the UK prime minister, when the back door was left open, as well as having a stand-off with the chief mouser at the famous address – Larry. Palmerston and Larry are said to have even had quite a serious cat fight that resulted in Palmerston damaging his ear and

Larry losing his collar. Palmerston also had quite the social media presence during his tenure, racking up an impressive 105,000 followers on Twitter.

In August 2020, Palmerston retired from his official government duties and moved to the countryside. His resignation was announced in a "letter" via Twitter, which explained he wanted to "spend more time relaxing away from the limelight" and claimed he was now climbing trees rather than "overhearing all the foreign dignitaries' conversations". He also claimed to have set up a "parallel network" for intelligence gathering during his time at the Foreign Office, praised his fellow "diplocats" and promised to always remain "an ambassador to the UK".

Palmerston now lives with a Foreign Office employee, out of the city where it's calm and quiet, and where Larry can't find him. He spends his days chasing wildlife and, according to reports from his new owner, partaking in daily yoga sessions.

PIPER PAWS: LIGHT IN THE DARKEST HOUR

Mother and daughter Patricia and Amanda were very close. Growing up, Amanda struggled to make friends at school and considered Patricia her best ally. Amanda was clumsy as a child, often falling over, but Patricia was skilled in catching her daughter when she tumbled. The doctor couldn't explain it, so Amanda spent a lot of her time in her mother's company.

When Amanda was 17, she was diagnosed with a neurological condition known as Dandy-Walker syndrome, a rare congenital brain condition. Her falls had in fact been symptoms. Dandy-Walker syndrome is often diagnosed alongside autism spectrum disorder (ASD) and suddenly a lot made sense to Amanda and Patricia.

Amanda said: "I lived in the same house with my mom forever. She looked after me and I never wanted to leave her. I did well at school but I had no friends outside – it was just her and me. I was socially awkward, I didn't like to be around other people much at all, except for my mom."

Some years later, Patricia was diagnosed with cancer, but after surgery and treatment was declared to be in remission. A few years after that, Amanda met Adam and the pair eventually got married, then moved in with Patricia, which worked out for everyone. Three years later, Patricia found out the cancer had returned and this time it had spread. Just one year later, Patricia tragically died.

On her deathbed, Patricia had made Adam promise to get Amanda a kitten. She had recently been devastated by the loss of her cat Sprinkles, who had lived with them for 16 years. Grief-stricken over her mother's death, Amanda struggled to function and couldn't leave the house. Adam decided the time was right to fulfil Patricia's dying wish.

Adam went to the local PURR animal shelter where a rescued cat had just given birth to four tiny black-and-white kittens. Adam adopted one for Amanda right away and took the little fluffball home to meet her new owner. Amanda was over the moon with her new pal, who was so small that she fitted into the palm of Amanda's hand. Amanda called the kitten Piper Paws – the Paws for her mother, whose full name had been Patricia Alane Warner Spencer.

With Piper at home, things felt brighter, lighter. Amanda had a sense of optimism she hadn't experienced in a long time and was sure Piper was responsible for the lift in her mood. Piper became quite inseparable from Amanda almost straight away. When Amanda thought about her mother and became upset, Piper would go to her and nuzzle her until she felt soothed. She would sleep in Amanda's arms and make her laugh on dark days with her kitten energy by hopping about the place.

Amanda said: "I believe that Piper Paws was sent by my mom to ease my grief and give me a reason to carry on after she died. She knew I would need someone special to get me through losing her. Although I had Adam, it was the first time I had ever been without Mom and it was ridiculously hard. I relied on her for so much. She loved me so hard and she was my greatest protector, so she left a gaping hole in my life. Mom knew that Piper Paws would fill that void and she was right. She gave me something to focus on other than my loss. I had to get up every morning to care for my kitten and to make sure that she was OK – I owed it to her not to collapse into my grief."

PIRAN: THE RESCUER CAT

Piran the black cat is a lucky omen and shared a strong bond with his owner, an 83-year-old Cornish woman.

Piran's owner went for a walk one warm summer evening in a maize field not far from where she lived in Cornwall, UK. However, on rugged terrain, she lost her footing, slipped and fell 69 feet through barbed wire and into a stream at the bottom of a ravine. There she lay, feeling somewhat battered and bruised and unable to get back up.

After a while, the woman's neighbour became aware of her absence and alerted others in the local vicinity. Neighbouring farmer Tamar Longmuir immediately began to search her farm from top to bottom to no avail, but she did notice Piran sitting at the gate to one of her maize fields, meowing incessantly.

The neighbours were aware of Piran's strong attachment to his owner, and when he began meowing and pacing back and forth in front of the gate Longmuir thought she had better investigate.

With 6 feet-high maize crops throughout the field and only a small track around the edge, Longmuir had to shout out her neighbour's name as she explored among the plants. Her cows joined in, thinking she was calling to them, but eventually she heard a faint human-sounding call in response. She followed the sound and soon realized her elderly neighbour must be at the bottom of the ravine.

Longmuir carefully traversed down the bank to her neighbour, who was unable to walk at this point, to assess the situation. Luckily she had only suffered minor injuries and seemed to have slipped through the barbed wire unharmed. "I came off worse than she did," said Longmuir.

Finding phone reception to make a call for help proved another challenge that saw the farmer climbing halfway up the bank and hanging off a tree branch waving her phone in the air in order to get one bar. She was eventually able to call the emergency services, which arrived swiftly and in droves.

According to Longmuir, some 12 vehicles and 25 crew from all the emergency services turned up to assist. It took 2 hours to help the elderly lady out of the ravine and back to the maize field, where she was placed in an air ambulance and flown to hospital. While she required some medical attention, she was said to be in very good spirits and suitably proud of her little Piran.

Longmuir said: "Without the cat waiting at the gate to that field, it could have been hours later that I or anyone else would have checked there."

Sounding the alarm when his owner was in grave danger led to the lady's rescue and no doubt saved her from coming to further harm. Piran's quick thinking was acknowledged when he was quite rightly nominated for a brave pet award. Local police also made mention of his bravery on their Facebook page by announcing: "Piran the cat saved the day!"

PONZU:
PAL TO PARROTS

Ponzu was a beautiful grey British shorthair cat living in Brooklyn, New York, USA. While you don't need to be a cat expert to know that they generally enjoy chasing birds, Ponzu had a different approach when it came to our avian friends.

Ponzu lived with his owners and their other animals – a tabby cat called Kimchi, a Shiba Inu dog called Tofu and a sun conure parrot called Mango. With names as delicious as these, it made sense that one of the pets' owner's, Chanan Aksornnan (aka Chef BaoBao) ran Southeast Asian restaurant Baoburg in Greenpoint, Brooklyn.

While the animals all shared a home and rubbed along with each other, it was Ponzu and Mango who shared a particularly special bond, sharing food and taking morning walks together. The pair would snuggle together at home, Mango cuddling up to Ponzu while he napped – they were just inseparable.

Mango would perch on Ponzu's shoulder as Chanan and her boyfriend strolled through the park together with their animals – Ponzu even enjoying it when Mango nipped on his ear – the sight delighted many people they encountered along the way.

Chanan said: "We need to learn from all these animals. They are different species, but they get along. They learn how to live together and how to fit into each other's lives."

The animals were an internet sensation, with Ponzu especially gathering an impressive following of fans and the Instagram account @ponzucoolcat racking up almost 50,000 followers.

PUDDING: A FRIEND TO DIABETICS

Pudding was a gloriously cuddly 9-kilogram ginger cat who was residing at the Door County Humane Society in Wisconsin, USA. When local resident Amy Jung popped in with her son Ethan to visit the cats, little did she know she would fall for one of them or that he would turn out to be something of a lifesaver.

When Amy saw Pudding it was love at first sight and leaving the shelter without him just didn't feel like an option. Pudding had been living there for a month along with his friend Wimsey. They had once shared an owner, but they had sadly died and left them without a carer.

Amy didn't hesitate to offer to take Wimsey home too – there was no way she was going to let the two cats be separated. The furry duo settled in straight away and made themselves at home as if they had always lived with Amy – she was overjoyed and the new pets felt like a perfect fit.

That night, Amy had a seizure in her sleep. She had suffered from Type 1 diabetes since she was a little girl and that night something was very wrong. Pudding sensed Amy's sleep-bound distress and jumped up onto her chest, nipping at her nose and pawing her to wake her up. Amy did so and shouted to Ethan in the next room, but he was fast asleep; she slipped into unconsciousness again.

Pudding jumped off Amy and ran into Ethan's room, leaping up onto Ethan, pawing at his face and meowing at the top of his tiny lungs. Ethan woke up and followed a howling Pudding into his mother's room, arriving just in time to prevent her from falling into a deadly diabetic coma. Amy remains convinced Pudding saved her life that night and that, without his intervention, she might not have woken up the next morning.

Pudding the lifesaver went on to train as a therapy animal and would sit next to Amy, learning to meow when her blood sugar was low and alert her to the fact.

RADEMENES:
THE COMFORTING CAT

Rademenes was a little black cat who hailed from Bydgoszcz in northern Poland. In 2014, he arrived at an animal shelter, just two months old and very poorly. He was suffering from a severe condition that attacked his upper respiratory tract and was in an awful lot of pain.

He had to fight hard for his life and was put into isolation while he battled the illness, losing much of his glossy black fur in the process. He eventually made a full recovery, thanks to the loving care of the staff at the shelter, including veterinarian Lucyna Kuziel-Zawalich who tended to him in his hour of need and refused to give up on the little cat when he was so unwell. Staff at the shelter were delighted that Rademenes had beaten the odds and was revitalized.

This particular shelter housed many animals – up to 200 at a time – and animals were always coming through the doors in a state of distress and in need of urgent medical attention. Rademenes became a feline member of staff, in a sense, and would always want to help a new arrival feel better. He would wrap his paws around the sick animals and embrace them.

When animals were resting following treatment or surgery, Rademenes would come to offer yet more support, sitting next to recovering dogs and cats, licking their ears and massaging their fur with his paws. Sometimes the little cat would sit next to a sick or wounded animal for hours, snuggling close to them.

Staff were overwhelmed at the affection Rademenes offered the other animals in their times of need and thought perhaps it was due to his experience of such a severe illness, which took him to the brink before he came back again.

His comforting nature gained him the nickname "nurse cat" and he became a permanent resident and mascot at the shelter, where he continued to offer support to his fellow animals if they ever needed a paw to hold or a supportive nuzzle.

LORD ROSCOE: THE NOBLE CAT

Roscoe was summoned to stately home Ham House in leafy Richmond upon Thames in London, UK, to do some serious mousing. Another cat had previously made its home in the grand, sprawling gardens of the seventeenth century National Trust manor house and unbeknown to staff was helping to control the mouse and squirrel population. When that cat passed away, the grounds quickly became overrun with rodents and something had to be done!

Assistant gardener Janette Slack-Smith went to local shelter Ginger Cat House Rescue to source a suitable replacement. Staff there knew immediately which cat would fit the bill. Black-and-white cat Roscoe was a regular escapee and not a fan of small spaces at all. The expansive grounds of Ham House would suit him perfectly, allowing him the freedom to roam and explore its many acres.

Roscoe slotted right into life at Ham House and he was a champion pest controller, helping to chase the squirrels away from the old statues and stop them from damaging the roofs of the vintage buildings by sharpening their teeth on the lead.

He also excelled at meeting, greeting and "volunteering" in the gift shop. He was so suited to life at the manor house that he was soon rewarded with a prestigious title and became Lord Roscoe of Ham House. Visitors to the property adore him and often come to the house asking if they can meet Lord Roscoe. Staff will then regularly radio around each other to find out where he was last spotted.

Lord Roscoe's celebrity status has seen him featured in news and magazine articles across the world, as well as on TV.

The lord of the manor may venture wherever he pleases on the property grounds, but he is not allowed to roam the corridors of the grand stately home. Instead, he lays his head to rest in the heated polytunnels in the garden or – in winter when it gets really chilly – is permitted to slumber in the staff quarters. He is, after all, a prominent member of staff and integral to the smooth running of the operation.

"He is fantastic and is really good at promoting Ham House," said Janette. "Everyone loves him – all of us, we adore him. The official line is we got him as a deterrent, but he is more of a lover, not a fighter."

RUSIK: THE SNIFFER CAT

Rusik was a stray Siamese cat living and wandering in the Stavropol region of south-western Russia, close to the Caspian Sea. Rusik used to sniff around the police checkpoints in the area when he was still a kitten. The officers were quite charmed by him, often feeding him scraps of sturgeon they had confiscated from smugglers.

An immense 95 per cent of the world's caviar hails from the Caspian Sea and smuggling is rife. Illegal sturgeon fishing is a huge problem for the authorities as there is much money to be made selling the sought-after roe in Moscow and elsewhere for huge profit. For this reason, many take their chances and the sturgeon population is at risk of being fished into extinction.

Rusik became a regular visitor to the checkpoints, aware there was an easy meal for him, and he was soon adopted by the staff. After so many scraps of sturgeon he developed a canny sense of the taste and scent of the fish, which gave the police an idea. Everyone's heard of sniffer dogs, but how about a sniffer cat? Especially one so familiar with the local fish – smugglers of which the authorities were trying to track down. We are used to sniffer dogs, but it's cats that have the keener sense of smell. The reason why canines get most sniffer work is that, unlike cats, they are easy to train and more willing to follow orders.

Rusik, however, turned out to be a dab hand in his new role and was so successful that he put the local sniffer dog out of a job. He would often alert police to stashes of illegally fished sturgeon hidden in vehicles passing through the checkpoints. The smugglers might have thought they were being clever with their well-thought-out hiding places, but Rusik always managed to sniff out the fish.

Rusik very sadly died when he was hit by a car driven by smugglers. Police couldn't be certain, but suspected a deliberate hit-and-run, with news having spread of the sniffer cat and his successful career of smuggler-catching. The checkpoint staff remembered the little cat fondly and never forgot his helpful nature.

SCARLETT: UNFALTERING LOVE

In 1996 in Brooklyn, New York, USA, an abandoned car dealer's premises caught fire. A local resident called the emergency services and firefighters were soon on the scene to control the blaze.

Just as the fire was almost put out, firefighter David Gianelli heard a faint meowing sound coming from beside the smouldering building. David followed the sound and discovered two tiny kittens. Further searches revealed three more tiny kittens across the street. A larger, badly burned cat, thought to be the mother, lay nearby.

The feline mother had clearly had to rescue her brood one at a time, making a separate journey back into the burning building for each one.

David tenderly placed all of the cats in a box together and witnessed the mother – despite her eyes being swollen shut – count her offspring by touching each one with her nose. David said once she had accounted for each one she lapsed into unconsciousness.

The cat family were sped to the North Shore Animal League facility at Port Washington, which housed an emergency room for animals and state-of-the-art veterinary hospital. Some years earlier, David had taken a badly burned dog to the facility and, despite fearing the worst considering the dog's dire condition, it had made a full recovery. He knew the mother and her babies were in the best of hands here.

The family were treated for smoke inhalation and burns, and spent some time in intensive care in an oxygen chamber. Mother and all but one of the kittens survived to make a full recovery. Staff at the facility decided to name the mother Scarlett due to the red patches of skin showing through her burned fur and the fact her actions had reminded them of those of Scarlett O'Hara in *Gone With the Wind*.

Along with her singed fur, poor Scarlett's ears were seriously burned, her eyelids swollen and her paws scorched. Luckily she retained her sight, but it was necessary to replace one of her eyelids.

The kittens were named Samsara, Tanuki, Oreo and Smokey, and when it came to rehoming the family offers came in their thousands from all around the world. The story of the mother cat's bravery had touched the hearts of millions of people globally and many of them wanted to be part of that story. The kittens were rehomed in pairs locally and Scarlett went to live with Karen Wellen in Brooklyn. She said: "I expected to see a scrawny, hairless cat, but she was gorgeous."

Scarlett needed to have eye cream applied three times a day, but apart from that she had a clean bill of health and thrived for another 12 years.

In 2008, Scarlett sadly passed away following a battle with several health problems not uncommon in older cats. When news of her death spread, the story was picked up by Reuters, which broadcast a huge image of Scarlett on its screen in Times Square, New York City. This came as a huge surprise to both Karen and the North Shore animal facility, and only went to show what a global impact Scarlett had had on people. The tale of the mother who returned to a burning building five times to ensure her babies would be saved pulled at the world's heartstrings.

Scarlett is forever remembered in an award created in her honour by the North Shore Animal League. The Scarlett Award for Animal Heroism is awarded to animals whose actions show great bravery that benefit humans or other animals. Recipients have included dogs who showed great courage in the wake of 9/11 and after Hurricane Katrina.

SCHNAUTZIE: A LUCKY ESCAPE

Greg and Trudy Guy from Great Falls, Montana, USA, had made the decision to buy a puppy. But it was a three-month-old rescue kitten that stole their hearts. Dreams of a family dog went out of the window once the little bundle of fur was in their sights. They named the kitten Schnautzie and took her home, where she settled in quickly.

Some six months later, in the early hours of a cold October morning, Trudy was woken up by a little paw patting her nose. She felt Schnautzie sitting on her chest and, somewhat bemused by the cat's behaviour, closed her eyes and drifted back to sleep.

Schnautzie didn't give up, however, and continued to paw at Trudy's face. This time she kept her eyes open and suddenly realized she could hear an unusual hissing sound. She woke up Greg to tell him about the strange sound, but he insisted it must be the neighbour's sprinkler. At this point Schnautzie had started sniffing incessantly at the air in the bedroom – Trudy was pretty sure the hissing sound wasn't coming from a sprinkler.

She followed the sound through the house and upon opening the bathroom door the hiss became much louder – not so much a hiss anymore but a roaring sound. The gas pipe outside the house had broken above the shut-off valve and toxic fumes were leaking into the basement of the couple's home.

Trudy grabbed Greg and Schnautzie and they charged out of the house as quickly as they could. Once safely outside, they called the emergency services – who would later confirm that Schnautzie was something of a life-saving wonder cat: she had alerted her owners just in time to a potentially lethal situation.

The Guys showered Schnautzie with treats and affection to thank her for her heroic actions. However, a few months later she was recognized by the Great Falls Animal Foundation and decorated with a Purple Paw award for bravery. Little Schnautzie quickly became something of a feline celebrity!

SCOOTER: THERAPIST TO MANY

Scooter was paralyzed from the waist down as a kitten, but one person refused to give up on him and he soon found his true calling in life.

In 2008, in Pittsburgh, Pennsylvania, Dr Betsy Kennon was examining the young kitten when she discovered the poor blighter was paralyzed. Life was certainly not going to be easy for a cat with only two working legs, let alone one who was so young. He had not yet had a chance to make an impact on anyone or make a case for his rehabilitation. Dr Kennon decided to vouch for him.

The clinic rallied around and, thanks to the generosity of its clients, raised more than $300 to build a mobility cart for the kitten, consisting of two wheels attached to a trolley on which his back legs rested and a harness that fixed around his stomach. The contraption was remarkable and enabled the little cat to walk around using his two front legs, pulling his wheels behind him.

Staff at the clinic decided Scooter was an apt name for the kitten and were delighted at how quickly he adjusted to life on wheels. Scooter needed further care, however, and being unable to use a litter tray by himself had to wear a nappy that needed changing twice a day.

Dr Kennon had hoped to find a loving home for Scooter and a carer who would cater for his needs. Sadly no such home could be found, so Scooter remained at the clinic.

Having spent much time in his company and being the one doing all the caring up until now, Dr Kennon saw something special in Scooter. She said: "It dawned on me that he was a real people kind of cat and possibly a good therapy cat."

And so it was decided that Scooter's true calling in life was to be a therapy cat. He became a regular visitor at several local nursing homes and brought hope to the patients. Dr Kennon said: "When patients see Scooter in his wheelcart, they think: 'If he can do it, so can I.' Animals don't think like we do: 'Poor me, I can't do this or I can't do that.' They just deal with the hand they've been dealt."

Scooter had a real impact as a therapist and did some life-changing work for one particular stroke victim who was not speaking. Dr Kennon recalled: "We put Sooter up onto her bed and he snuggled right up to her. And don't you know, she petted him, she opened her eyes and she was talking to him. And I thought, that's really cool. When I turned around, the recreational therapist and nurse were both in tears."

In 2012 Scooter was awarded the ASPCA Cat of the Year Award. Dr Kennon concluded: "He brings patients a little bit of happiness, a little bit of joy and a little bit of hope that things are going to get better."

Did you know?

A study carried out by scientists at Kyoto University in Japan found that cats who live with other cats are able to identify and learn each other's names. The research looked at 48 cats who either cohabited with at least two other felines in a home or a cat café. The mogs were monitored separately and each shown a photograph of one of their feline pals; the scientists then called the cat's name along with a series of unrelated names. It was found that in most cases the cat would stare at the picture for longer when the correct name was called.

SCOUT: REACHING UP FROM ROCK BOTTOM

Josh Marino was serving for the US army in southwest Baghdad, Iraq, when a mortar attack caused an explosion a mere 9 feet away from him. He suffered a traumatic brain injury and PTSD.

On his return home to post-combat deployment, he was stationed at Fort Riley in Kansas. Josh was suffering from severe anxiety, a lack of focus and sporadic memory loss. He said: "A lot of us come home without realizing we're bringing the war with us, with an invisible wound that nobody can see."

One night he was so depressed he planned to take his own life, wrote a note on his computer and stepped outside his house for what he told himself was to be his final cigarette.

Josh said: "That's when I heard a little meow. This little black-and-white kitten was walking out of the bushes. He walked up, started rubbing up against my leg and let me pet him. I burst into tears. Maybe he knew that there was something I couldn't quite handle. I stopped thinking about all of my problems and started thinking about his problems and what I could do to help him."

Josh would call to the little cat every day and feed him. The kitten eventually began to recognize his voice and would trot right over for his nightly meal. "He gave me something to look forward to every day. He didn't see my flaws or imperfections," Josh said, "I felt safe."

One day after work, Josh headed out to his yard to call for the cat, but he didn't come. Josh called and called and waited, but there was no sign. He realized the cat was no longer around and was devastated.

Time passed and Josh started dating Becky, whom he had known at high school. A few months into their relationship they were walking past the Fort Riley Stray Animal Shelter and an "adopt-a-thon" was taking place. They decided to go inside and have a look.

Walking through the rows of crates, a black-and-white paw reached out from between the bars and started tapping Josh on the arm. He looked inside and saw that same little black-and-white cat. He said: "I opened up that cage and I pulled him out and held him tight. I signed the paperwork then and there and I named him Scout."

Eventually Josh and Becky got married, and Josh moved to Pittsburgh to live with her and her three cats, where life in their house was "a lot of fun". "Scout made me want to better myself," he said. He quit smoking, went out on his bike more and ate healthier. He went back to school and got a master's degree, which led him to a career in mental health helping other veterans. "Now I'm serving in a different uniform," he said.

One day Scout was acting sluggishly and didn't bound to the door to greet Josh like he usually did. After taking him to the vet it was confirmed he had feline leukaemia. He was given enough medication to give Josh and Becky a couple of weeks in which to spend time with him, say their goodbyes and spoil him in any way they could.

One sad morning Scout couldn't catch his breath. Becky drove him to the vet, but he passed away in Josh's arms in the back of the car on the way there.

"Even before he was my cat, before he even knew me that well, he saved my life," Josh said. "He put me on a different path. I don't go a single day without thinking about him. He saved me, all I did was the paperwork."

SIMON: A VITAL CREW MEMBER

Back in 1948, British warship HMS *Amethyst* was stationed in Hong Kong. Seventeen-year-old crew member George Hickinbottom happened upon a skinny monochrome cat kicking about in the dockyard and decided to smuggle him on board.

George named the cat Simon and he was soon merrily accepted by the rest of the crew, who saw him as a valuable weapon against a growing rat population on the lower decks.

In April 1949, *Amethyst* was travelling up the Yangtze River on its way from Shanghai to Nanjing, to relieve HMS *Consort* from duty. *Consort* had been guarding the British Embassy there from the perils of the Chinese Civil War that was currently in full swing between the Kuomintang and the Chinese Communists.

In what was later to become known as the Yangtze Incident, *Amethyst* came under a 101-day siege from the People's Liberation Army. All that time Simon was busy below decks culling the rats that were piling onto the vessel from the riverbanks, attracted to the crew's dwindling food supplies. While under siege there was no way to restock and Simon's job was one of the most important aboard the ship.

At the beginning of the siege, Simon had been wounded by some shrapnel when the captain's cabin had been attacked and the commander killed. When he was discovered, Simon was rushed to the medical bay and had four pieces of shrapnel removed, but the doctor on board didn't expect him to last the night.

Simon defied the diagnosis and bounced back quickly, returning to his rat-killing duties. Simon would also regularly visit the medical bay where many teenage soldiers lay wounded and recuperating, and would help to lift their spirits.

The ship finally escaped the siege in November 1949. News of Simon's actions aboard the *Amethyst* had spread and he was greeted like a celebrity at each port the ship stopped at on the way home to the UK. When the ship arrived in Plymouth, the crew received a hero's welcome and Simon had received so many letters of admiration that a naval officer had to deal with the fan mail.

He might have been famous, but rules were rules and Simon had to be quarantined when he arrived back in the UK. Tragically, he died there after three weeks from an infection caused by his shrapnel wounds.

Simon received a funeral with full military honours at the PDSA (People's Dispensary for Sick Animals) Animal Cemetery in Ilford, Essex. Hundreds turned up to pay their respects to a truly special cat. The entire crew of HMS *Amethyst* attended, forever grateful to Simon for helping save their lives by protecting their precious food stores while under siege.

Simon was posthumously awarded the PDSA Dickin Medal, which is the highest award any animal can receive while serving in the military. A total of 71 animals have been awarded the Dickin Medal, but Simon is the only cat to have ever achieved this prestigious accolade. Other recipients include Winkie the carrier pigeon, the very first recipient, for carrying important messages for the RAF in 1942 and saving the lives of a downed air crew; Upstart the police horse, who served in Bethnal Green during World War Two and was able to stay calm and not bolt despite being showered with debris from a nearby bomb; and Rip the crossbreed terrier who became the Air Raid Patrol's first official search-and-rescue dog during World War Two, saving the lives of more than a hundred people during the London Blitz.

When a ceremony was held in 2007 to commemorate Simon's bravery, commander Stewart Hett, who had been on board *Amethyst* with Simon, said: "Simon's company and expertise as a rat catcher were invaluable during the months we were held captive. During a terrifying time, he helped boost the morale of so many young sailors, some of whom had seen their friends killed. Simon is still remembered with great affection."

Director general of the PDSA Marilyn Rydström said: "The power of animals to support and sustain morale in times of conflict can never be underestimated."

SNOW WHITE:
HEMINGWAY'S SIX-TOED CAT

Writer Ernest Hemingway was one of America's literary greats, giving the world *The Old Man and the Sea*, *For Whom the Bell Tolls* and *A Farewell to Arms*, among other books.

Notoriety surrounded the author and, as well as being famous for his heavy drinking – "The only time it isn't good for you is when you write or fight", he once said – he also partook in activities such as bull-running and boxing.

However, Hemingway clearly had a gentle side and was also a great lover of cats. He kept many throughout his life – some reports claim up to 70 at a time – and once said of his feline companions: "A cat has absolute emotional honesty: human beings, for one reason or another, may hide their feelings, but a cat does not."

His most famous pet a was white cat, Snowball, a gift bestowed upon Hemingway by ship captain Stanley Dexter visiting Key West, Florida, USA, where Hemingway lived; Snowball was quickly renamed Snow White by Hemingway's children. Snow White was an oddity in that she was a polydactyl feline, meaning she possessed six toes. Hemingway had admired the cat's extra digits and so the captain had said he must have her. Never to be neutered, Snow White roamed all over Key West and it wasn't long before Hemingway's estate was close to being overrun with litters of cats with six digits, all boasting their own little thumbs.

Upon Hemingway's death in 1961, his house was converted into the Ernest Hemingway Home & Museum, which has become as famous for its cat population as its former writer resident. Most of the cats are polydactyls and thought to be descended from Snow White. Hemingway named each member of his army of cats after a famous person, so that tradition is carried on to this day.

SPARE: MORE LIFE TO LIVE

Nicky and David lived in a ground-floor flat in east London, UK, with their cats Storm and Hex. They would leave a big bowl of food in the kitchen every night, which was always polished off by the morning, and yet their furry companions didn't seem to be putting on any weight.

The back door, protected by iron bars, was left open every night so the cats could come and go. Could this be part of the mystery? The couple set up a webcam and the following day, all was revealed. The camera footage showed a huge black-and-white cat squeezing in through the bars and stealing Storm and Hex's dinner. The intruder was feral and odd-looking.

Nicky said: "It was pretty ugly, like it had been made up of lots of spare parts that had been sewn together. We watched as it sneaked in and ate all the food, then disappeared again into the night."

The couple decided to let the cat, whom they nicknamed "Spare", keep on eating the food. For the next year or so he would come for a midnight feast and Storm and Hex even took a shine to him.

In February 2015, a major storm raged across the UK. While Storm, Hex and their owners were safely inside, Spare stumbled into the room and crept underneath the sofa. He appeared so unwell that Nicky wondered if he was about to die. He refused to be touched and simply cried softly.

The couple called the Celia Hammond Animal Trust who came to pick up Spare. Despite his weakened state he put up quite a fight! The charity called later to inform Nicky and David that he was 15 to 20 years old, with rotten teeth, a urinary tract infection and a serious virus. The fact he was still alive was a miracle; if he continued to survive, he would have six months to a year left. The charity said they would give him all the medical attention he needed, along with his vaccinations, if Nicky and David agreed to let him live in their garden and feed him.

After two months, Spare was released by the charity and Nicky put him in their spare bedroom. When she let him out he vanished, but three weeks later he returned – much to everyone's relief.

Nicky and David moved house and took Spare with them. For several weeks he refused to come out from under the bed in the spare room. Nicky would read him stories and push plates of tuna under the bed.

The following year Nicky suffered a miscarriage and was heartbroken. On her return from hospital, she climbed into bed and slept. When she woke up Spare was sitting on the end of her bed, staring at her. Until now he had not been into her bedroom and had never even let Nicky stroke him.

Nicky said: "From then on he slept every single night at the end of the bed on my side. It only took a couple more days until he inched closer and nuzzled me. This was the cat who, although he had never hurt me or David, would try to slap us with his paw if we went too close."

This closeness continued and Spare grew ever more loving toward his rescuers. Nicky said: "I would wake up in the morning with him pushing his nose under my arm and he would often sleep next to my back, as if he had to be close to me. I like to think that he sensed my grief and deep loss and he wanted to help."

A month later Nicky and David got married and received a little white kitten as a wedding gift. Spare was besotted with it, and the kitten loved him too. Eighteen months later Nicky gave birth to a daughter. Spare fell in love with her too and the pair became great friends.

In December 2020, sadly Spare passed away. Nicky scattered his ashes in her garden among the forget-me-nots and felt forever grateful they had taken a chance on this funny feral cat. He clearly still had so much life to live and love to give.

SYLVESTER: THE PERSISTENT PERSIAN

When Patricia Kerr adopted five-year-old part-Persian ginger stray Sylvester, it was company she had in mind – she didn't for one minute dream he might save her life one day.

Ninety-year-old Patricia lived in a small town in New Zealand and had brought Sylvester home to be her buddy. He was a shy cat, only allowing Patricia to pet him and fleeing when other humans were around.

This made it all the more unusual when Patricia's neighbours opened the door one morning to find Sylvester on their doorstep meowing loudly. Shirley and Monte Mason were taken aback to find the usually nervous and reclusive cat clamouring for their attention.

Wondering what might have caused the cat such distress, the Masons headed to Patricia's house to see what was going on. There was no answer, so they thought perhaps she had gone out. The Masons were about to head out themselves, so they decided to check in on Patricia later to make sure everything was alright.

When the Masons got back, Sylvester was still meowing loudly. Her neighbours noticed Patricia had not put her bins out as usual and so they rang the doorbell once more and called her on the phone. When there was no answer to either, they grew worried and called the emergency services.

The police arrived and broke into the house. Patricia was in the bath, unable to get herself out; the water had grown quite cold and she was in a state of hypothermia. She was rushed to hospital, where she was treated for the condition. Patricia made a full recovery and returned home. The Masons were told they had raised the alarm just in time; however, they credited Sylvester with alerting them to his owner's distressing situation.

TABOR: A TALE OF TWO OWNERS

Michael King was spending most of his nights sleeping in a UPS loading bay in a rundown area of Portland, Oregon, USA, when one evening he made a new friend.

Formerly, Michael had worked as a chef, but after losing his partner to AIDS he went on the road. He sadly fell into homelessness, alcoholism and depression.

Michael was in no fit state to take on new responsibilities, but when he came across a bedraggled, dirty and injured cat, he felt an urge to take care of the poorly feline. Michael spent his last few dollars on food for the cat and resolved to nurture her back to health.

He named her Tabor after the café where she had approached him and the pair became firm friends, spending their days together in the city. Michael referred to Tabor as "a rainbow in a dark world" and when he felt down, Tabor knew how to comfort him. Michael had found someone to love and care for, who would also eventually help him to get sober as well as deal with his past traumas and losses.

When it grew too cold in Portland, Tabor would perch on Michael's backpack and they'd go on the road together, relying on the kindness of strangers, who were endeared to help the travelling homeless man with his kitty companion. While living beneath a tree on a California beach the pair had to fend off coyotes; while in Montana they had encounters with bears and angry armed locals.

Tabor did her fair share of life-saving too. While the pair were camping in Yosemite National Park in California, Michael had a few drinks and fell asleep by the fire. Tabor yowled and screeched to alert Michael to the fact his sleeping bag was on fire and had burned away up to his knees.

One day Michael took Tabor to a veterinarian in Montana and was surprised to learn she was microchipped, meaning she had an owner. Michael was heartbroken at the thought of giving up Tabor; he felt equally sad for her owner who must have been pining for her for the past 10 months and for Tabor, who had likely missed her family. He made the difficult decision to return to Portland and reunite Tabor with her original owner.

Ron Buss had indeed been pining for his beloved cat, whom he knew as Mata Hairi (Mata for short), more than Michael could have known. He had had several breakdowns and consulted cat psychics to try to find out what had happened to his much-loved cat.

Ron had rescued Mata and her four siblings when they were week-old kittens after finding them abandoned under a neighbour's porch. He had bottle-fed them all until they were old enough to be rehomed and had then kept two of them. He named Mata's brother Creto and treated the cats as if they were his children, cooking for them and taking them everywhere with him. He would also play the guitar to his cats and sing them Beatles songs – after all, the band's members were cat lovers.

When Mata disappeared and didn't return, Ron feared the worst. Creto also longed for his sister and would sit on the porch every night waiting for her to come home.

Michael and Tabor finally made it back to Portland and Ron was reunited with his beloved pet. Tabor was distressed at having to leave Michael's side – he had been her companion, her everything for the past year. Ron was upset to see his cat so sad and remembered how much little Mata had loved it when he played music to her. He said that playing 'And I Love Her' by the Beatles to Mata helped her realize who he was and where she was supposed to be.

Michael meanwhile, never forgot Tabor and the effect she had on him. He went on to take in a series of strays on the road and eventually found a permanent companion in a puppy he named Abbey Road, who stuck by his side as they travelled the coast together.

In 2017, Britt Collins wrote the book *Strays* about Michael and Tabor's remarkable journey home.

TAMA: SAVIOUR OF THE RAILWAY

Tama was a Japanese calico cat widely credited with saving a failing railway line. The Kishigawa Line in Japan's Wakayama prefecture runs through a mountainous and rural area, famous for its temples and pilgrimage trails. In the late 1990s, Tama was a young kitten living near Kishi station, the last of the 14 stops on the 8.9-mile line that takes commuters from rural stations into Wakayama City at the line's terminus. Tama was popular with the commuters and often affectionately referred to as Kishi's "stationmaster".

By the mid-2000s, fewer people were using the railway line and lack of funding left its future hanging in the balance. By 2006 none of the stations along the line were staffed and an announcement was made that the railway was to be abolished. Local residents rallied together and approached the president of another train company, the Wakayama Electric Railway, to ask him to revive the line.

This is where Tama stepped in. The much-loved cat had been cared for by a shopkeeper local to Kishi station; however, when he moved on he had asked the railway to care for the calico cat. Mitsunobu Kojima, president of the electric railway, had apparently always been a dog person, but when he met Tama that all changed. He fell in love with her and adopted her right away.

With the Kishigawa Line up and running again, in 2007 Tama was officially named stationmaster of Kishi station and presented with a tiny, customized stationmaster's hat. She became the face of the railway, appearing in advertising campaigns and on television. Her presence was ever felt at the station, too, and she would greet passengers by the gates or from behind the glass in the ticket office. Kishi station even boasts a souvenir shop, largely devoted to ephemera adorned with Tama's image – from stickers and T-shirts, to food and keyrings.

Tama's rise didn't stop there. In 2008, she was promoted to super stationmaster and received a knighthood from the governor of Wakayama prefecture. In 2009, the station building was redesigned in the shape of Tama's head, with ears protruding from the roof, windows serving as cat's eyes and a mouth acting as the door. Tourists flooded to the station to see her and it is estimated by the Wakayama Electric Railway that the number of passengers on the line has increased by almost 300,000 annually since 2006.

Tama-mania continued and 2010 saw the birth of the Tamaden railway. The trains on the Kishigawa line were redesigned in homage to Tama, with paw prints and illustrations of the famous calico cat adorning the exterior. The interiors were lined with shelves of children's books and fitted with a PA system that plays a recording of Tama purring whenever the doors open at a station.

The themed trains don't stop at cats, either. The Kishigawa line also boasts a strawberry train and a pickled plum train – fruits for which Wakayama is well known – which attract scores of tourists year-round.

In 2015, Tama died at the age of 16 having become something of a household name across Japan. Her funeral was held at Kishi station and was attended by thousands of mourners, who brought flowers and tins of tuna. In remembrance, Tama was officially renamed the honourable eternal stationmaster and a shrine to her was created on the platform where she used to appear.

Tama's legacy is strong on the Kishigawa line and feline stationmasters play an ever-important role in the running of the railway. Tama was succeeded by other cats including Nitama (translating as "Tama two"), Santama ("Tama three") and Yontama (you guessed it, "Tama four").

Gone but not forgotten.

Did you know?

Throughout history, cats have been considered spiritual and a symbol of good luck in Japan. The famous waving-cat figurines are thought to bring good fortune to businesses, which is why they can often be spotted in shop windows the world over. Shrines and statues dedicated to cats can be found in Japan, and there are more than ten "cat islands" that have become hugely popular tourist destinations, where hundreds of kitties roam freely. Then there are the famous cat cafés in Tokyo; and let's not forget fictional character Hello Kitty who has been wildly popular since the 1970s.

TARA: FIERCELY PROTECTIVE

Tara the tabby cat lived in Bakersfield, California, USA, with the Triantafilo family, having followed them home from the park one day in 2008 and deciding she wanted to stay. The Triantafilos were happy with that and, upon making the necessary investigations, Tara became part of the family.

A few years later, baby Jeremy was born and Tara became his protector. She used to sleep next to his crib and the pair always shared a close and special bond. The family lived a reasonably quiet life until one day Tara became an internet sensation.

In 2015, four-year-old Jeremy had been riding his little bicycle on the family driveway when a large dog appeared from behind their car and went straight for the little boy's leg. In a completely unprovoked attack – the dog approached Jeremy from behind – the dog took Jeremy's leg in his jaws, pulling him from his bike, and began to shake him around.

Fortunately, the ordeal didn't last too long as Tara the family cat hurled herself at the dog, slamming into its body and chasing the attacker away. In footage captured by the family's video surveillance cameras, Jeremy's mother Erica can be seen rushing to his aid. She said: "He was just playing outside and I was watering the plants. Next thing I know the dog was just there and it was shaking him. Before I could even get there, my cat clobbered him. She saved the day, chased him away and then came back to him after the dog was gone."

Jeremy was taken to hospital and needed ten stitches in his leg to help heal the wound. According to reports the dog was quarantined following the attack.

Jeremy's father Roger uploaded the video clip of the toddler being attacked and then rescued and within a couple of days it had clocked up 4 million views. Tara was hailed as a most remarkable cat.

Erica said: "To have her, with no regard for her own life, fly at the dog to protect Jeremy – I've never seen anything like that before."

In 2016, Tara was presented with a very special award. The Society for the Prevention of Cruelty to Animals Los Angeles presented her with the Hero Dog annual award – however, for the first time in the accolade's 33-year history they changed the title and had the word 'Cat' etched onto the trophy instead. Tara was the very first feline recipient of the award and the Triantafilo family were beyond proud of their hero cat.

Jeremy said: "She's my hero."

TILLY: THE CANOEING CAT

Long-haired calico cat Tilly loves nothing more than getting out on the water with her owner Holly Hancock. The pair live in Norfolk, UK, and can regularly be seen out and about on the Norfolk Broads sailing in Holly's canoe.

Holly has been taking Tilly out since she was a five-month-old kitten and she took to life on the water immediately. She calls Tilly her "adventure buddy" and now she joins Holly at least once or twice a week when the weather is fine.

Holly said: "Tilly has always been interested in what we are doing, following us around and doing things cats don't normally do. One day we thought we would try to take her out on the canoe and she absolutely loved it. She loves looking at all the wildlife. She's definitely a special cat."

Trips take the pair of them along peaceful waterways, where the duo bask in the abundant nature, listening to birdsong and enjoying the heavenly sunsets. Passers-by often do a double take when they see a cat on board, but are always charmed and often want to say hello or take a picture.

Holly keeps a leash and a carrier on board in case Tilly gets scared on the water and needs somewhere to hide, but it's rare for that to happen.

Part Norwegian forest cat, Tilly is primarily an indoor cat, so Holly's pleased she can be out in the fresh air when on the water.

Holly said: "She is so intrigued by all the wildlife she usually just sits and watches. Seeing her brightens up everyone's day. People are so surprised to see a cat on a boat, whereas you see lots of dogs out on the water. I sometimes think Tilly thinks she's a dog."

TOLDO: LOYAL PAST THE END

When Toldo's owner died, his loyalty never waned. The grey-and-white tomcat lived in the village of Montagnana near Florence, Italy, with his owners Ada and Reno Iozelli. In 2011, Reno sadly died and was buried in the village cemetery.

On the day of the funeral, Toldo could be seen following the procession through the streets, all the way to the graveside. Three-year-old Toldo had been with his owners since he was a kitten and had been particularly close to Reno. The family members watched lovingly as Toldo attended the funeral of his lost friend, but a few days later they were even more astounded at the little cat's displays of loyalty and affection toward his departed owner.

On the day after the funeral, a sprig of acacia appeared on Reno's grave; later on that evening Toldo was found at the grave, standing vigil. Toldo began to visit the cemetery regularly and each time he did he brought something with him to place on the grave of his owner.

Ada said: "Sometimes he comes with me and sometimes he goes on his own. He brings little twigs, leaves, toothpicks, plastic cups – a bit of everything really. The whole town knows about him now. He loved my husband. It was something else! Now it's just me, my daughter and my son-in-law, and he's very affectionate with us too."

TOMMY: THE PHONE-SAVVY CAT

Gary Rosheisen lived in Columbus, Ohio, USA, with his orange-and-brown-striped cat Tommy. Tommy was Gary's best friend and had been living with him for around three years.

Gary suffered from osteoporosis, which led to him having mini-strokes from time to time. His balance was also affected by the condition, so he used a wheelchair at all times. Tommy was a great source of calm to Gary and kept him company in their home. The friendly feline even helped to lower his owner's blood pressure.

Gary liked to spend time trying to train Tommy to do useful things, such as dialling 911 should this ever be required. That said, he was never sure if Tommy was learning from these training sessions as he often seemed not to be paying attention.

One night, Gary fell out of his wheelchair and was unable to lift himself up. He usually wore a medical alert necklace with a button to summon paramedics in an emergency, but he wasn't wearing it that day. There was also an emergency cord above his bed that he could pull in the event of such an emergency, but he was too far away to reach it. He felt helpless.

Gary wasn't lying on the floor for very long before the police arrived at his apartment – he couldn't believe it. How had they known he needed assistance? He hadn't been able to alert them. The police explained: they had received a 911 call that was traced back to Gary's number, but they couldn't hear anyone on the other end of the line. They called back to check in case the call had been accidental, but there was no response so they had arrived to check if anyone needed help.

When they arrived the police had found Tommy lying next to the telephone on the living room floor and Gary lying on the floor next to his wheelchair. Everyone was confused, but Gary explained that Tommy must have made the call.

One police officer at the scene said: "I know it sounds kind of weird… But there wasn't any other possible explanation!"

Gary was thrilled his cat had saved the day and that he had taught him to do it. All the time he had spent teaching Tommy to press the speed-dial button for 911 had paid off – no matter how disinterested he had been at the time. The speed-dial button sat just above the speakerphone button, so it's not beyond the realms of possibility that Tommy had been able to push it with his paw.

Gary said: "He's my hero."

TOMMY POSTOFFICE: THE MAILROOM CAT

While modern-day post offices are secured against pests, their forebears would keep a cat to stop rodents from destroying the mail.

But back in the early twentieth century, in the post office in Hartford, Connecticut, USA, one morning a mailbag was emptied and a tiny black kitten tumbled out. The little thing had been smothered by the mail and was barely alive, after being knocked around in the bag on the train from New York City.

A postal worker warmed up some milk and fed it to the kitten from a bottle, while the post office spaniel Koko licked the kitten to revive it.

Hartford Post Office contacted its New York counterpart to see if it was missing a kitten – indeed it was. The New York post office cat had given birth to a litter and had put one of her babies in bed in a mailbag while she went on the hunt for the rest of her brood. However, the mailbag was then filled with mail and sent out of state.

The minuscule feline already had a name – Tommy Postoffice – and the New York staff thought it fitting he should follow in his mother's footsteps and continue the family tradition of post office mousing, taking up a job in Hartford.

As Tommy grew, he developed a white tuxedo and took his role as head of pest control very seriously. On occasion he would sit at the delivery window and "stamp" each outgoing letter with his paw.

One day Tommy strayed from his mail-protection duties, and was found to have ripped open a package and was rolling in its contents. However, the staff soon forgave him when they realized the package had been full of catnip. Word got out about the much-loved post office cat's discovery and, from then on, Tommy regularly received letters from his fans, addressed to him and stuffed with catnip.

Postal workers taught Tommy tricks, which he would often perform at charity events to earn money for the post office, and he won the award for general intelligence at the Hartford Cat Show.

When the Hartford post office engineer was on holiday, his temporary replacement was unfortunately a bad-tempered man who disliked cats. He ordered Tommy out of the furnace room, where he liked to go to keep warm, but one night he found his way back in. The cat jumped onto the engineer's shoulder – as he was prone to do with the regular cat-loving engineer – as he was opening his sandwiches to beg for a bite, but this caused the stand-in to become so startled that he picked up Tommy and threw him into the boiler pit, full of hot coals.

Tommy jumped out, but was badly hurt. The coals had burned off a lot of his fur, part of his tail, his claws and the pads of his feet. Poor Tommy cried in pain and the other postal workers came running to his aid. They tended to his wounds and cared for him tenderly in the days that followed. They feared the worst for their dearly loved feline friend, but eventually he began to show signs of recovery and drank a little milk. After ten days he ate a little food and very slowly, bit by bit, he started to get better. His fur and whiskers grew back and eventually he was his old self once more.

Post office staff and the police had wanted to talk to the stand-in engineer about what had happened, but he had slipped away straight after the incident and was never to be heard of or seen again.

Before the attack, Tommy had turned up at the post office one day carrying a tiny black-and-white kitten that looked just like him. The tiny fluffball had become his apprentice and had duly stepped up to Tommy's duties around the post office while he was in recovery. Once his health was restored, however, Tommy wanted the post office spotlight all to himself, so the young protégé was relocated elsewhere.

Tommy lived a long life and was immortalized in a biography dedicated to his service in 1905 – *The Adventures of Tommy Postoffice*, by Gabrielle E. Jackson.

TOTO: SOMETHING IN THE AIR

In Italy there once lived a little cat named Toto who was thought to have had a premonition of sorts, saving the lives of his owners from a horrific natural disaster.

Gianni and his wife Irma lived in the village of San Sebastiano al Vesuvio in Naples, located on the western slopes of Mount Vesuvius.

One day in March 1944, the couple noticed Toto behaving strangely. He was out of sorts and skittish – persuading him into the house when it got dark was no easy task. Eventually he settled and everyone went to bed.

At midnight, Gianni was awoken by Toto scratching at his cheek. Not only had he been disturbed from his slumber, but Toto had hurt Gianni and he was angry with the cat. He wanted to send the cat out of the bedroom, but Irma was concerned about Toto's unusual behaviour. This was hugely out of character for the usually sweet and docile kitty.

Irma suggested that Toto might be trying to tell them something and perhaps they should take his behaviour seriously. Luckily, Gianni bought in to Irma's superstitions.

The pair packed a few things and headed out of the house to where Irma's sister lived, taking Toto with them.

Within an hour, Mount Vesuvius had erupted and the entire town of San Sebastiano al Vesuvio was destroyed. A river of lava half a mile wide flowed down the hillside, also destroying the neighbouring villages of Massa di Somma, Ottaviano and part of San Giorgio a Cremano.

In Gianni and Irma's village, 30 people were killed – that number would have been 32 if it weren't for the actions of a brave little cat.

While many at the time believed that Toto had predicted the future and saved his owners from their doom, in recent years a more plausible explanation has emerged. Scientists have suggested that there is a surge in positively charged ions in the air just before a volcanic eruption and that cats are able to detect these subtle variations, as well as changes in magnetic fields.

Toto might not have "predicted" the eruption of Mount Vesuvius, but he knew something was wrong and acted in the only way he knew how.

Did you know?

In 1979 in northern California, USA, there was a very powerful earthquake along the Calaveras Fault — so strong that it shook buildings over 124 miles away. Before the earthquake, many cat owners had reported strange behaviour in their pets. Could the cats have predicted what scientific equipment had been unable to detect? This is thought to be due to the vomeronasal organ on the roof of a cat's mouth that allows them to feel, taste and smell the air around them. This allows them to carefully examine it, accessing far more information than the human nose might provide.

TRIM: THE INTREPID EXPLORER

Way back in 1797 a stowaway cat from London, UK, gave birth to a litter of kittens aboard HMS *Reliance* while the ship made its journey from the Cape of Good Hope in South Africa to Australia's Botany Bay. The kittens found their sea legs in no time, developing an impressive sense of balance and being quite unbothered by the water itself – unusual for cats.

One kitten stood out from the litter – black, with a white star on his chest, he was described as having feet that seemed to have been "dipped in snow". English explorer Matthew Flinders was aboard the ship and named the kitten Trim after the butler in *Tristram Shandy* by Laurence Sterne, due to the little fluffball's "great fidelity and affection".

Trim once fell overboard, but was quite unaffected by the experience, simply swimming back to the ship when a rope was thrown to him. Flinders said Trim "took hold of it like a man and ran up it like a cat".

Flinders even wrote an essay in homage to Trim: *A Biographical Tribute to Trim the Cat*; only published in 1973, this had been lurking in the archives of the National Maritime Museum for many years before it was rediscovered.

According to Flinders: "He grew up to be one of the finest animals I ever saw, his tail was long, large and bushy... his head was small and round – his physiognomy bespoke intelligence and confidence – his whiskers were long and graceful and his ears were cropped in a beautiful curve."

Trim was something of a born performer, regularly entertaining the ship's crew with tricks such as jumping over someone's clasped hands and lying flat on his back until he was granted permission to rise. When the rigging was hoisted, Trim was up there like a shot, able to climb to the top faster than anyone else on board.

At dinner time, Trim would be the first to arrive at the captain's table and wait for everyone to be served before requesting a small bite to eat from each attendee. If anyone refused, he would wait until their back was turned before taking a morsel for himself.

Trim was a trusty companion to Flinders on several voyages, including his mission to circumnavigate the coastline of Australia and in the process establish it as a continent, rather than a collection of islands as had previously been presumed. He made the same trip once more, in 1802–1803 aboard the *Porpoise*; however, the ship was wrecked when it collided with a coral reef. Flinders swam to shore with Trim and the other survivors, where they struggled to stay alive before being rescued two months later by HMS *Cumberland*.

Sadly, the next part of their journey took a tragic turn. England had declared war on France, so when the *Cumberland* arrived at the port in the French colony of Mauritius, Flinders was immediately accused of being a spy and thrown in prison. Unable to take Trim with him, he arranged for him to go and live with a local family. Soon after, while still behind bars, Flinders heard that Trim had gone missing. He was broken-hearted at the thought of his lost cat and said: "To the memory of Trim, the best and most illustrious of his race, the most affectionate of friends, faithful of servants, and best of creatures. He made the tour of the globe, and a voyage to Australia, which he circumnavigated, and he was ever the delight and pleasure of his fellow passengers."

Flinders was incarcerated for seven years before finally being granted permission to return home to England. With a heavy heart and still mourning the loss of his travelling companion, he set sail.

Flinders and Trim have both been immortalized in sculpture by John Cornwell, who created a bronze statue in 1996 that sits on a window ledge of the Mitchell Library in Sydney, directly behind a statue of Flinders that was erected in 1925. Another statue of Flinders was installed in his hometown of Donnington, Lincolnshire, UK, in the marketplace. Sat at his feet, of course, is Trim.

VELMA: THE SOCIALITE CAT

British comedian Suzi Ruffell lives in London, UK, with her ginger, tortoiseshell and white Cornish rex cat Velma. When the Covid-19 pandemic closed all venues, performers had to find another way to pay the bills. Suzi sprang into action and began working on two podcasts – *Like Minded Friends* (with fellow comedian Tom Allen) and *Out with Suzi Ruffell* – from her home in London.

Working from home – and during the UK lockdowns confined to her abode for most of the day – meant she could be around Velma pretty much 24/7. Suzi said: "She loves to be with me. She will sit on my shoulder when I'm working or on a Zoom call."

Having originally wanted a dog, but deeming the idea impractical due to the amount of time she often spent away from home, Suzi decided to research cat breeds that displayed the most similar behaviour to canines. Cornish rexes are known for being friendly and outgoing – even around strangers – and are often described as "the border collie of the cat world". As one of the more sociable of the cat breeds, it made sense to Suzi that in lieu of a hound she should opt for a cat that was, like her, a born entertainer. And so she found her feline companion, naming her Velma after Velma Kelly from the musical *Chicago*.

One thing Velma isn't short of is personality, bounding to the door – much like a dog – to greet Suzi when she arrives home. Suzi said: "She loves visitors who come round, and especially male visitors. When I have to be away, I have a male cat-sitter for her and she has a big crush on him!"

Rather than meowing, Velma cries like a baby when she wants something and "needs just as much attention as a human baby". An indoor cat, she occasionally sneaks onto the balcony, but appears terrified if she spots another cat. She also isn't one for hunting, at the most catching a fly now and again, so being indoors suits her down to the ground.

As many people did, Suzi found much comfort in her pet during the pandemic and various lockdowns. She said: "When I'm feeling down, I just have to listen to this little purring creature beside me and I feel better. Whenever I was feeling sad, Velma never left my side. I'm sure she sensed that something was wrong. She is very special and I wouldn't be without her."

VENKMAN, RAYMOND, EGON AND GOZER: WHO YOU GONNA CALL?

The Empirical Brewery in Chicago, USA, had a serious rat problem. The critters were munching their way through the company's grain stores and causing supply problems. With Chicago home to one of the largest city rodent populations in the world, the struggle was major. The Empirical's staff tried everything to get rid of the rats, but just had no luck in getting the numbers down. They couldn't keep up with the rats' ability to create more rats and it was killing business.

Then someone had a brainwave. The brewery looked to Chicago's Tree House Humane Society to help them with their predicament. The shelter rescued feral cats from the streets of Chicago and, after neutering and vaccinating them, trained them up to be pest controllers for businesses and private residences around the city. In return for their rodent-removal services, the cats simply required food and shelter.

This arrangement worked for everyone – the businesses got pest controllers who were expert hunters, and the cats who were not suitable to be rehomed as pets could do a job and be looked after away from the dangers of the streets.

The Empirical Brewery adopted four cats to help them with their severe rat problem. The three males and one female had been part of a colony found in an abandoned parking lot in the city, so as they were known to each other they were likely used to working as part of a team. The three male cats were named Venkman, Raymond and Egon, and the female was named Gozer – all characters from the blockbuster 1980s film *Ghostbusters*. It was no surprise, then, that the crew of cats was nicknamed "the Rat-busters".

It wasn't long before the Rat-busters had seen off all the rats at the brewery and it's fair to say the staff were thrilled. So thrilled, in fact, that they constructed a multi-level home for the cats in the brewery space as a thank you, to allow them to lounge around when not on duty.

The cats didn't just see off the rats, they boosted the profile of the brewery with some happily received PR. Multiple media outlets published stories on the new feline presence at the brewery and no doubt won the business a few extra beer sales in the process.

Operations manager Jim Ruffato said: "We've definitely got more attention for the cats than the beer."

WILLOW: THE VAN CAT

In 2015, Rich East's long-term relationship broke up. Along with being sick of working in the corporate world for the past decade, this propelled him to do something to shake himself out of the funk he was in. Rich was living in Hobart, Tasmania, an island state of Australia, and thought perhaps a trip – an epic trip – might be the cure he needed.

Unwilling to leave his cat Willow behind, he decided the perfect itinerary for the two of them would involve visiting all eight states and territories of Australia. They would also complete the "loop" of the country's coastline – often referred to as "the big lap". With more than 80 per cent of the population of Australia living within 30 miles of the coast, staying close to the edge allows a traveller to see nearly all of the cultural and natural attractions the country has to offer.

Having rescued jet-black cat Willow from a shelter in Hobart, Rich said: "I made a promise to look after her when I adopted her and I wasn't going back on it, just because I was looking for something else in life."

Rich was serious about his new life on the road that stretched out ahead of him. He sold his house and most of his possessions, packed up his campervan and headed off.

Circumnavigating Australia was ambitious for a cat, but laid back Willow was up for coming along for the ride. Highlights for the pair included sailing the Great Barrier

Reef, spending the summer at the Dorrigo Plateau mountain range and driving a 620-mile gravel road from Bourketown to Queensland and up to the Northern Territory.

A typical day on the road for the travelling companions involved sightseeing, eating, napping, driving a short distance to the next camp, before cooking and eating some more and getting some well-earned rest – before doing it all over again the next day. The duo took the travelling in their stride, in no rush to get to the end of their journey.

Rich described Willow as "curious" and "cautious" and she would generally stay on her leash until she felt comfortable with her new surroundings. After ensuring the area was safe for her, Rich would then allow her to roam – but she never really ventured very far from the van. And if Rich ever couldn't locate Willow by sight or call, he was able to track her via her radio frequency collar.

When Rich was driving, Willow travelled in a cat carrier for safety and she liked to lounge on top of the campervan during the day or under some blankets on the back seat. At night, she could often be found curled up and purring at Rich's feet.

The two completed their loop of Australia, but their adventures didn't stop there. In 2016, halfway through said loop, Rich met Steph in Perth. Referring to her as "the love of my life", Steph joined them on the road and took up the role of "chief cat attendant" – a job she takes seriously and "the road trip of a lifetime quickly turned into an endless summer". Rich wrote on his website vancatmeow.com: "In

June 2019, after getting a non-opposable thumbs up from Willow, I asked Steph to marry me."

The trio now lives what Rich calls a "nomadic lifestyle" and he says, "anyone who lives on an island will tell you, if you keep driving in one direction long enough you will eventually hit the coast again."

Did you know?

Possibly one of the most incredible journeys to be made by a feline was that of stray Parisian cat Félicette on 18 October 1963, when she was sent into space by the French. She is the only cat to have ever left the Earth's atmosphere and was sent on the journey with electrodes attached to her skull so her neurological activity could be monitored. She travelled 99 miles into space on a 15-minute flight before descending back to Earth, where she landed safely.

YANG: FREEDOM TO ROAM

Ginger, green-eyed cat Yang has been making the five-minute journey to his local hospital nearly every day for almost seven years to cheer up staff and patients. Hexham General Hospital in Northumberland, UK, described Yang as a "ray of sunshine in the darkest days" for everyone at the hospital.

Twelve-year-old Yang can often be found lying at the entrance to the hospital or sitting on one of the visitors' wheelchairs, and helps to relax visitors and patients.

Modern matron Jane Ferguson, who works at Hexham Hospital, said: "When patients come to the hospital site they're really anxious and worried. They might feel extremely vulnerable and Yang just brings a sense of calm and peacefulness to everybody he meets."

The comforting cat has been put forward for a PDSA Order of Merit, often referred to as the "animal OBE". In May 2023 he was recognized by Hexham Town Council as an animal that embodies "the spirit of this caring town" and awarded a certificate, a special key medallion and the honour of Freedom to Roam. In a special ceremony, Yang was dubbed a "top cat" and "the ultimate volunteer".

A spokesperson for the council said Yang had "dedicated years of service to this hospital and distracts people from their worries, giving purrs and strokes free at the point of use in the NHS."

Yang's owner, Glynis Bell, couldn't be more "proud of Yang and to be able to go through all of this with him".

She told the *Chronicle* newspaper: "He'll watch certain people as they're coming in or out [of the hospital] and he just beelines to them. If he sees them sitting on a seat he'll run over to them and put his two front paws on their lap, and just look up at them as if to say 'I'm here, do you want to talk?' It's so amazing to sit and watch."

Hospital visitor Alison Galilian said Yang's presence has made returning to the hospital, which holds difficult memories for her, easier. "I would walk up to the doors of the hospital with a very heavy heart and a lump in my throat. Seeing Yang waiting inside the hospital doors, I'd sit down for a cuddle.

"He really helped lift my spirits and reminded me that life carries on. I have been receiving physiotherapy treatment on a regular basis so always look forward to a cuddle and chat with Yang before going inside. Having Yang there has made my visits much easier to manage now."

ZEBBY: SMOOTH OPERATOR

Zebby is an incredibly helpful cat and his owner Genevieve Moss just wouldn't be without him.

Black-and-white two-year-old support cat Zebby provides a vital service for his deaf owner by alerting her when the phone is ringing and helping out around the house.

When he hears an important sound, Zebby will gently tap his paw on Genevieve's face so she knows to insert her hearing aid. She said: "Without my hearing aid, I can't hear anything, but now I have Zebby to help me."

Despite having no formal training, Zebby has learned to assist Genevieve – even fetching the post in his mouth and locating her slippers for her.

If Zebby hears an unusual noise in the night, he will paw at Genevieve's head until she wakes up to investigate and if someone knocks at the door, he paces in front of her to let her know.

In July 2023, Zebby was honoured for his good work when he won the top accolade at the National Cat Awards, run by UK charity Cats Protection, when he was named National Cat of the Year 2023. Cat behaviour officer at the charity Sammie Ravenscroft said: "Although Zebby hasn't had any formal training for the role he has taken up, he has found something that must be special for him too as he continues to do it, whether it be a head rub or a tasty treat when he has done well. Either way, Zebby is a perfect example of a cat that is truly remarkable."

Genevieve was overjoyed at the recognition received by her special little helper cat: "I am so proud of Zebby for showing the world how intuitive and caring cats can be, and what a positive effect they can have on people's lives. I can't imagine life without Zebby and I'm over the moon that he's been honoured in the National Cat Awards. Living on my own and being deaf means life could be lonely, but not with Zebby around – he's my hero."

Did you know?

In 1876, the postal service in the city of Liège, Belgium, thought they could train cats to deliver mail. First they tested their homing instincts by taking 37 cats individually 20 miles outside the city and setting them free. The first arrived home less than five hours later and after 24 hours all 37 cats had returned to their homes. The post office thought this proved the cats could successfully carry mail in waterproof bags around their necks and deliver it around the city and neighbouring villages. The system didn't catch on.

CONCLUSION

From evidence of a sixth sense to heart-warming tales of rescue against the odds and the most remarkable stories of survival, you've seen it all on these pages. Cats are and will no doubt continue to be one of the world's best loved pets, but they are so much more than that. They offer companionship when there is no other support, protection from – at times – huge threats, affection when it is needed the most, support throughout the struggles of life and even, as we've seen here, become travel partners on epic journeys across great distances.

Cats offer loyalty, love, friendship and care – and, as these pages attest, close to every remarkable cat an equally remarkable human can be found too.

RESOURCES AND INFORMATION

If you enjoyed these stories, here are details of some books, websites and podcasts you may be interested in.

Books

A Streetcat Named Bob: And How He Saved My Life by James Bowen

Strays: A Lost Cat, A Homeless Man and Their Journey Across America by Britt Collins

Felix the Railway Cat by Kate Moore

Full Steam Ahead, Felix: Adventures of a Famous Station Cat and Her Kitten Apprentice by Kate Moore

Nala's World: One Man, His Rescue Cat and a Bike Ride Around the Globe by Dean Nicholson

Websites

Cat Blood Donors
www.catblooddonors.com

Cat Chat
The Cat Rescue Resource (UK). www.catchat.org

Cats Protection (UK)
www.cats.org.uk

The Cat Site
www.thecatsite.com

Crafty Cat
www.craftycat.co.uk

International Cat Care
www.icatcare.org

Pets as Therapy
www.petsastherapy.org

North Shore Animal League America
www.animalleague.org

American Society for the Prevention of Cruelty to Animals (ASPCA)
www.aspca.org

Podcasts
Nine Lives with Dr Kat
Cattitude
The Purrrcast
The Community Cats
The Catmaste Chronicles

Dog Tales

UPLIFTING STORIES OF TRUE CANINE COMPANIONSHIP

Ben Holt

DOG TALES

Uplifting Stories of True Canine Companionship

Ben Holt

ISBN: 978-1-83799-284-3

Paperback

This collection of heart-warming stories shares true accounts of some extra-special pups and celebrates the many ways dogs uplift and enrich our lives every day.

Dive into these pages to meet some of the most incredible dogs and puppies who have touched the lives of their owners in unforgettable ways. From loyal service dogs who have helped their owners through some of life's toughest challenges, to playful puppies who bring joy to every moment, the furry friends featured in this heart-warming collection of stories will leave you feeling uplifted and inspired.

Whether you're a dog lover or simply need a dose of positivity, the stories inside are sure to raise your spirits. Filled with tales of courage, love and loyalty, this book is here to remind you of the unbreakable bond between dogs and humans. So settle in with your furry friend and get ready to be inspired by the stories of these amazing pups!

SUPER CATS

*True Tales
of Extraordinary Felines*

ASHLEY MORGAN

SUPER CATS

True Tales of Extraordinary Felines

Ashley Morgan

ISBN: 978-1-80007-688-4

Paperback

Meet some of the world's most incredible real-life cat heroes in this awesome compendium of true stories, including:

- Scarlett, the brave mother who went into a burning building five times to rescue her kittens.
- Emily, the cat who survived an epic journey across the Atlantic trapped in a shipping container from America to France.
- Oscar, the care-home cat who predicts when residents are about to pass on and comforts them in their final hours.

Whether they're testing the boundaries of their nine lives or demonstrating unusual talents, cats are always full of surprises. In *Super Cats*, prepare to meet the most surprising of all.

From loyal companions who put their lives at risk to help others to intuitive cats who detected danger when no one else did, these extraordinary felines will capture your heart and make you marvel at their astonishing powers.